Stand As A King
&
Rule As A Queen

And The Two Shall Become One...

"Two are better than one, because they have a good return for their labor: If either of them falls down, one can help the other up." (Ecclesiastes 4:9-10, NIV)

HARRISON MUNGAL

Stand As A King and Rule As A Queen

Copyright © 2025 Harrison S. Mungal

All rights reserved. Neither this publication nor any part of this publication may be reproduced or transmitted in any form or by any means, electronic or mechanical, including photocopying, recording or any information storage and retrieval system, without permission in writing from the author.

Contact author via email:
hsmungal@hotmail.com
info@agetoage.ca
www.agetoage.ca
www.harrisonmungal.com
www.harrisonmungalbooks.com
Facebook: Harrison Mungal
Twitter: AgeToAgeInc1
LinkedIn: Harrison Mungal, Ph.D., PsyD
YouTube: Harrison Mungal
Phone: 905-533-1334

ABOUT
HARRISON *and* KATHLEEN

Harrison and Kathleen Mungal have built their lives on a foundation of faith, love, and a deep commitment to family. With over 34 years of a strong and successful marriage, they have nurtured a beautiful family that includes seven children, in-laws, and multiple grandchildren. Their devotion to the Lord is at the heart of their journey, and they actively serve in their local churches, carrying forward their passion for ministry.

Together, Harrison and Kathleen have played pivotal roles in church planting, pastoral leadership, and missionary work. As missionaries during the War in Croatia from 1994 to 1997, they ministered in challenging circumstances, spreading the gospel with unwavering faith. Over the years, they pastored in four churches, planted two congregations, and established a Bible college, which they led for over a decade. Their transition into mental health and addictions counseling was a natural extension of their heart for healing, combining their pastoral experience with practical tools to support individuals and families.

Their ministry spans the globe, speaking in churches worldwide on topics related to relationships, marriage, parenting, mental health, addictions, and the intersection of spirituality and psychology. Harrison is widely respected for his ability to blend biblical truths with scientific insights, bringing a unique "psychology twist" to his therapeutic approach. He explains that God created us as Body, Soul (mind, will, and emotions), and Spirit, and while physical and spiritual support are crucial, "the soul is where people are wounded and is in need of healing."

Harrison's expertise has been sought after by numerous media outlets, including appearances on *700 Club Canada* and *100 Huntley Street*. His wisdom has been shared in prestigious institutions, such as the Attorney General of Canada, police departments, hospitals, community agencies, and churches. His contributions have earned him widespread recognition from local authorities, police departments, mayors, community leaders, and countless families.

Through their life's work, Harrison and Kathleen have demonstrated an unwavering commitment to service—integrating faith, wisdom, and compassion to positively impact individuals, couples, and families. Their journey stands as a testament to the power of love, faith, and the pursuit of healing for those in need.

Table of Contents

INTRODUCTION	7
STAND AS A KING AND RULE AS A QUEEN	13
TWO ARE BETTER THAN ONE	19
WHO IS MORE IMPORTANT?	27
ROLES AND RESPONSIBILITY	33
CHARACTER AND PERSONALITIES	43
EMBRACING DIFFERENCES	51
EMBRACE A TEAM MINDSET	57
UNITY IN LEADERSHIP	63
ACCOUNTABILITY	69
DEALING WITH STRUGGLES	75
OVERCOMING CHALLENGES	81
NOT SEEING THINGS EYE TO EYE	89
EMOTIONS AND RATIONALIZATIONS	97
STRENGTHS AND WEAKNESSES	105
APPRECIATE PRESSURE	113
SKILLS, EXPERIENCE AND KNOWLEDGE	119
COMPLIMENT AND COMPROMISE	127
AVOID PROBLEMS DOMINATING	135
YOUR PROBLEM YOUR ISSUE	141
THE EGGSHELL ENVIRONMENT	151

AVOID EMOTIONAL BULLYING 159
WINDOW OF TOLERANCE 167
SHOCK THE BRAIN 175
MATURE THE MIND 181
A FILING CARBINET.. 189
PUT CLOSURE TO YOUR PAST 195
CONCLUSION 203
REFERENCES 209

INTRODUCTION

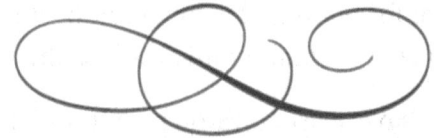

Throughout history, some royal marriages were mere political arrangements—calculated alliances designed to secure power. But William III and Mary II of England were different. Their reign from 1689 to 1694 was more than just leadership; it was a partnership, proving that ruling a kingdom—or building a marriage—requires balance, trust, and the ability to lead together rather than alone. Together, William and Mary proved that a king does not have to overshadow his queen, and a queen does not have to diminish herself to support her king. They embraced their differences—one leading battles, the other leading governance—and their reign became one of the most influential in history.

This book explores the power of teamwork in marriage, like William III and Mary II of England to show that when two people work together, they can achieve remarkable things. Their reign proves that leadership and love are strongest when built on partnership, trust, and mutual respect. Just as they ruled side by side, modern couples can thrive by embracing unity—supporting each other's strengths, sharing

INTRODUCTION

responsibilities, and recognizing that two individuals, when truly connected, can become one.

A marriage, like a kingdom, flourishes when both partners stand together, not in competition, but in collaboration. Marriage is a sacred and powerful union—one where two individuals come together not just in love, but in purpose, vision, and mutual support. It is a partnership designed to flourish when both people embrace their unique roles and responsibilities.

Stand As A King and Rule As A Queen will take you on a journey with Kathleen and me as we uncover the principles and practices that shaped our blueprint for building healthy relationships—one that is now being embraced by couples and families across the world.

Kathleen and I have learned through our years of experience that two are better than one. The journey of marriage is filled with ups and downs, victories and challenges, but when two people walk side by side in strength and understanding, their bond grows deeper and their efforts yield good returns. Too often, relationships falter because individuals focus on their differences as obstacles rather than opportunities. The most successful marriages thrive when partners learn to rule together as a king and queen, understanding their value and function within their relationship while honouring each other's strengths.

Every great kingdom requires structure, vision, leadership, and teamwork. A marriage is no different. By building your lives together with intentionality and purpose, you create a strong foundation for success. But this foundation requires more than just love—it needs unity, accountability, trust, emotional intelligence, and a willingness to embrace challenges rather than letting them dominate.

A common misconception in marriage is the idea that one person holds greater significance than the other. Many couples struggle with power dynamics, believing that one spouse must lead while the other follows. But in truth, the strength of a marriage lies in mutual empowerment.

A king without a queen lacks wisdom, emotional depth, and insight. A queen without a king lacks stability, security, and vision. Kathleen and I have discovered that true power comes from understanding your roles and embracing them with confidence. The king is responsible for setting the direction and protecting the family, while the queen nurtures, refines, and ensures that the emotional and relational aspects remain strong. These roles are not hierarchical—they are complementary.

Successful couples understand that they do not have to be everything for each other. Instead, they support each other in the areas where they are naturally strong and provide grace where they may be weak. A king does not need to be perfect; he needs to lead with wisdom and humility. A queen does not need to carry all the burdens alone; she needs to rule with grace and discernment.

One of the greatest challenges couples face is learning to appreciate differences rather than seeing them as roadblocks. Every person brings unique personality traits, perspectives, and experiences into a marriage. Learning how to balance introverted and extroverted personalities, rational and emotional perspectives, structured and spontaneous approaches is crucial for a thriving relationship.

Early in our marriage, Kathleen and I struggled with these differences. I approached decisions with immediate action, while she preferred reflection and careful thought. I sought social engagement and external solutions, while she found strength in quiet introspection. At first, these differences led to misunderstandings. But over time, we learned to use our strengths to complement each other rather than compete against one another.

Embracing a team mindset transforms relationships. Instead of fighting for control, couples who work together build an environment of trust and collaboration. Unity in leadership does not mean agreeing

INTRODUCTION

on everything—it means making decisions that serve the family's best interests rather than individual desires. Ruling together as a team requires accountability, ensuring that both partners take responsibility for their actions and choices without blaming or dismissing the other.

Every relationship faces obstacles. Financial pressures, parenting conflicts, personal insecurities, and past wounds all have the potential to strain a marriage. But challenges do not have to break a relationship—they can strengthen it if handled with wisdom and grace.

One valuable lessons Kathleen and I learned was the importance of separating the problem from the person. Too often, couples allow frustrations to overshadow their love, treating disagreements as personal attacks rather than opportunities for growth. Problem-solving together rather than blaming each other creates a pathway for resolution and healing.

Not seeing things eye to eye is inevitable in marriage. No two people will always agree on everything. But the power of agreeing to disagree lies in respecting each other's perspectives without allowing differences to create division. Emotional intelligence plays a vital role in this—learning to balance emotions and rational thought ensures that conversations remain constructive rather than reactive.

Many couples struggle because they do not fully recognize the strengths and weaknesses they bring into the relationship. The truth is, nothing is wasted—every challenge, every lesson, every moment of pressure serves as a catalyst for growth.

Kathleen and I learned that pressure refines character. The difficulties we faced as a couple and as parents helped us mature, sharpen our understanding, and strengthen our ability to support each other. We discovered that our skills, experience, and knowledge evolved as we committed to maturing our minds rather than staying stuck in old patterns of thinking.

Compromise and compliments became keys to our thriving marriage. Learning to appreciate the beauty of our differences and the value of working together helped us rule our family with confidence and joy.

One risks in marriage is allowing problems to overshadow love. Financial stress, external pressures, and unhealed wounds can dominate a relationship if couples do not actively choose to let love be the guiding force.

Kathleen and I made the conscious decision early on that our problems would never become our spouse's issue to carry alone. A healthy marriage does not place one person as the "fixer" while the other struggles in silence. Instead, partners work together, supporting each other without making problems the dominant focus of the relationship.

Choosing love over conflict means avoiding the eggshell environment, where tension silences communication. It means understanding whether the fight is truly worth the casualty, avoiding emotional bullying, and ensuring that disagreements do not spiral into unnecessary battles.

The mind is like a filing cabinet, storing every experience, thought, and emotion we encounter. Couples must be intentional about filling their memory cabinets with positive cards rather than negative ones.

Kathleen and I found that when we focused on gratitude, forgiveness, and trust, our relationship flourished. We learned to shock the brain by responding with love instead of reacting with frustration. Letting go of past mistakes, maturing our perspective, and committing to closure and moving forward helped us build a kingdom that reflects unity, strength, and unwavering love.

Standing as a king and ruling as a queen is not about power—it is about embracing responsibility, fostering love, and creating a life built on mutual respect and partnership. Marriage is strongest when partners

INTRODUCTION

work together, building a kingdom that reflects wisdom, grace, and unwavering commitment.

Kathleen and I invite you to embark on this journey of growth, learning how to rule together, embrace your roles, and master the art of standing side by side in confidence and love. The challenges will come, but the rewards will far outweigh them. Together, you have the power to build your lives with purpose, maturity, and unwavering devotion.

Let's begin.

STAND AS A KING AND RULE AS A QUEEN

Build Your Lives Together To Rule Your Kingdom

Marriage can be likened to a kingdom, with the husband and wife taking on the roles of a king and queen. This analogy isn't about dominance or rigid authority—it's about partnership, shared responsibility, and leveraging each other's strengths to create a thriving union. Together, the king and queen establish and protect their "castle," a metaphor for their marriage and family life.

Kathleen and I had to learn how to implement this dynamic in our own lives. Like many couples, we discovered that working together and embracing our unique roles was the only way to harness the full potential of our partnership. When we stopped fighting to take on roles we weren't suited for and instead focused on complementing each other, we found a balance that brought harmony and strength to our relationship.

The journey wasn't easy; it required intentional effort, humility, and a willingness to learn from our mistakes. But through this process, we saw the power we had as a couple when we worked as a team. We had to work together as a teamwork in raising a family. Standing as a king and ruling as a queen is essential for creating a strong and united "castle."

As the king, the husband takes on the role of spiritual leader in the marriage and family. This doesn't mean ruling with an iron fist or asserting dominance—it means leading with love, wisdom, and humility. In our relationship, I had to learn that being the "king" wasn't about controlling Kathleen or making all the decisions. Instead, it was about setting the spiritual tone for our household, protecting our family, and ensuring that our actions aligned with our shared values.

One of the king's primary responsibilities is to provide direction and vision for the family. This involves making thoughtful decisions, planning for the future, and leading by example. For me, this meant taking responsibility to discuss our finances, creating goals that aligned with our values, and ensuring that our family's priorities were centered on faith, love, and unity. It also meant acknowledging my limitations and seeking Kathleen's input and wisdom when faced with difficult decisions.

Another vital aspect of the king's role is to serve as a protector. In a figurative sense, this means standing guard over the "castle" to shield it from external threats, whether they're financial challenges, emotional stressors, or conflicts that threaten to disrupt the family's harmony. As the spiritual head, the king ensures that the home remains a safe haven— a place where love, trust, and respect thrive.

Research highlights the importance of shared leadership in families, noting that when one partner assumes a leadership role rooted in service and humility, it strengthens the relationship and fosters collaboration (Markman & Rhoades, 2020). For me, learning to lead as a servant-leader was transformative, teaching me that true leadership is about uplifting and empowering my partner and family.

As the queen, the wife brings a unique set of strengths to the marriage that complements the king's role. Kathleen embraced this position with grace, using her gifts and talents to nurture our family, create emotional stability, and support our shared goals. Her role wasn't about submission or passivity—it was about stepping into her strengths to create balance and harmony in our relationship.

One of Kathleen's greatest strengths as the queen was her ability to nurture and connect emotionally. She created an environment of warmth and love in our home, ensuring that our children felt valued, heard, and cared for. Her empathy and emotional intelligence complemented my more pragmatic approach, helping us navigate challenges with both heart and mind. For example, while I focused on practical solutions to financial challenges, Kathleen reminded me of the importance of emotional well-being and the need to prioritize family time.

The queen's role also involves being a source of wisdom and insight. Kathleen's ability to think deeply about our family's needs often provided clarity during moments of uncertainty. She wasn't afraid to voice her opinions or challenge my perspective when she felt strongly about an issue, and her input often led to better decisions. In this way, she ruled alongside me, bringing balance to our partnership.

Studies show that when partners value and leverage each other's strengths, it leads to greater relationship satisfaction and resilience (Barton et al., 2021). Kathleen's role as the queen wasn't about standing in the background—it was about standing beside me, using her gifts to strengthen our family and build a foundation of unity.

In the analogy of the king and queen, the "castle" represents the marriage and family—the life that the couple builds together. Protecting the castle requires teamwork, shared responsibility, and a commitment to acting in the family's best interest. For Kathleen and me, this meant recognizing that threats to the castle didn't always come from external sources—they often came from within.

One of the greatest lessons we learned was the importance of addressing conflicts and challenges together rather than allowing them to create division. When financial stress or parenting disagreements arose, we reminded ourselves that the problem wasn't Kathleen or me—it was the issue at hand. By working as a team, we were able to tackle challenges without letting them weaken the foundation of our castle.

Another aspect of protecting the castle is setting boundaries and establishing priorities. For us, this meant saying no to things that didn't align with our values and making time for the things that mattered most—our relationship, our faith, and our family. It also meant being intentional about nurturing our marriage, ensuring that our love remained strong even as we juggled the demands of daily life.

One of the most powerful aspects of the king and queen dynamic is the ability to work together as a team. Kathleen and I discovered that when we aligned our efforts and supported each other's strengths, we were able to accomplish far more than we could individually. This teamwork extended to every area of our lives, from raising our children to managing our household to pursuing our dreams.

For example, when I decided to go back to school in my 30s to pursue a new career path, Kathleen stepped in to provide the emotional and practical support I needed to succeed. She managed the household during my busy seasons, offering encouragement and understanding when the pressure felt overwhelming. In turn, I supported Kathleen in her passions and pursuits, creating space for her to explore her talents and grow as an individual.

Teamwork also means sharing responsibilities in a way that honours each partner's strengths. Kathleen and I divided tasks based on what we were best at rather than adhering to traditional gender roles. This approach allowed us to maximize our efficiency and reduce stress, creating a more balanced partnership.

Research underscores the importance of teamwork in relationships, noting that couples who approach challenges collaboratively are more likely to experience long-term satisfaction and stability (Finkel et al., 2017). For Kathleen and me, working together wasn't just a strategy—it was a mindset that shaped every aspect of our lives.

The roles of a king and queen are not about power or control—they are about partnership and purpose. Standing as a king and ruling as a queen allows couples to create a relationship that is rooted in mutual respect, shared responsibility, and unwavering commitment. Here are some of the reasons why embracing these roles is essential:

1. **Strengthens the Relationship:** When couples embrace their unique strengths and work together, they build a relationship that is resilient and harmonious.
2. **Promotes Growth:** The king and queen dynamic encourages personal and relational growth, as both partners are empowered to step into their full potential.
3. **Protects the Family:** By working together to protect the "castle," couples create a safe and nurturing environment for their children and themselves.
4. **Fosters Unity:** The king and queen model emphasizes collaboration and teamwork, ensuring that both partners are aligned in their goals and values.
5. **Reflects Love and Respect:** Standing as a king and ruling as a queen demonstrates a commitment to loving and respecting each other as equals, creating a foundation for lasting intimacy and trust.

The roles of a king and queen in marriage are not about titles or rigid expectations—they are about creating a partnership that thrives on mutual support, shared responsibility, and unwavering love. Kathleen and I have learned that by embracing these roles, we are able to build a "castle" that reflects our values, protects our family, and strengthens our bond.

As couples navigate the journey of marriage and family life, they have the opportunity to step into these roles and work together as a team. By leveraging each other's strengths, addressing challenges collaboratively, and prioritizing love and respect, they can create a kingdom that stands strong through the test of time.

TWO ARE BETTER THAN ONE

Good Returns For Your Labour

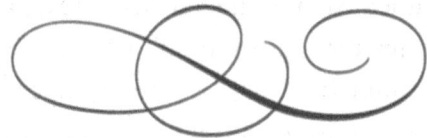

Throughout history, we see that to stand as a king, he must have a queen—not just as a figure beside him, but as an essential partner in ruling, building, and creating a lasting legacy. It has always been understood that two are better than one, for together, they strengthen each other, produce after their kind, and pass wisdom and heritage to the next generation. No king can truly stand alone—he needs his queen to rule with him, ensuring that their kingdom thrives through unity, shared vision, and mutual support.

Kathleen and I have embraced this truth in our own lives, knowing that to be strong individuals, a strong couple, and a strong family, we need each other. Having a partner by our side brings balance, offers perspectives we might have missed, and provides clarity where our own understanding falls short. Just as a king and queen work side by side to govern well, we have learned that love, wisdom, and shared leadership

TWO ARE BETTER THAN ONE

in marriage bring good returns for our labour, allowing us to build a lasting legacy for the generations that follow.

Kathleen and I have come to realize one of the most powerful truths in marriage—two are better than one. There is an undeniable strength in partnership, a depth of understanding that grows when two people commit to building their lives together. Marriage is not about one person carrying the full weight alone; it is about sharing burdens, celebrating victories, and supporting each other through every challenge. When we learned to work as a team rather than individuals navigating separate paths, we saw firsthand the good returns for our labour—a relationship rooted in trust, companionship, and resilience.

Through the years, we have faced moments where life tested our unity. There were times when financial struggles, parenting challenges, or personal insecurities threatened to pull us in different directions. But when we reminded ourselves that we are stronger together, we found solutions that worked not for one, but for both of us. The efforts we put into communication, sacrifice, and understanding have always returned to us in the form of a deeper connection, a stronger marriage, and a family built on love.

It is easy to see a marriage as a balance sheet—taking stock of what each person brings to the relationship, weighing expectations against contributions. But true partnership is not about keeping score—it is about working in harmony. Kathleen and I don't look at our efforts as separate; we see them as combined forces, reinforcing a foundation that will hold firm through every season of life. This mindset has brought rich rewards, teaching us that love multiplies when it is nurtured, and trust deepens when it is honoured.

Through the years, we've realized that success in marriage isn't about keeping score or proving who contributes more—it's about celebrating the efforts we both put into our relationship. Some seasons require me to carry more weight, while in others, she leads the way. But through it all, we stand side by side, knowing that everything we build together benefits us both, our family, and the legacy we leave behind.

A kingdom thrives when its leaders work in harmony, and marriage is no different. Kathleen and I have cultivated a relationship rooted in trust, communication, and shared responsibility, understanding that our greatest strength is not in our individual abilities but in our commitment to standing together. And when we look back at all that we have built—the stability, the love, the growth—we see proof that two truly are better than one. Standing together, ruling together—this is the essence of a kingdom built on love, where the returns are far greater than we ever imagined.

Kathleen and I have always felt a calling to build our marriage on a foundation of faith. Through the years, certain scriptures have deeply resonated with us, guiding us as we navigate the complexities of life together. These sacred words have not only encouraged us but affirmed that we are on the right path, walking in alignment with God's design for partnership. As we reflect on these scriptures, we are reminded of profound truths about teamwork, unity, and the shared calling to build a life centered on love, respect, and purpose.

The Bible says, *"Two are better than one, because they have a good return for their labor: If either of them falls down, one can help the other up."* (Ecclesiastes 4:9–10, NIV).

Kathleen and I discovered the depth of this scripture early in our marriage, particularly during moments of hardship. It taught us that the power of partnership lies in its ability to strengthen, uplift, and support.

The concept of "two being better than one" emphasizes synergy—the idea that when two people work together, their combined effort achieves results far beyond what either could accomplish alone. This isn't just a practical principle; it's deeply relational. In life, there are times when one of us feels weak or discouraged, unable to carry the weight of a situation. Ecclesiastes reassures us that in those moments, the other is there to step in, to offer strength, encouragement, and hope. Kathleen has been my steadfast supporter, my anchor, and my hand to hold when the road seemed uncertain. Together, we rise from the falls and press forward, trusting God's plan for our union.

This scripture also reminds us that partnership isn't about perfection—it's about presence. It's about being there for one another in the messiness of life, offering grace and comfort in times of need. Kathleen and I have come to cherish this truth, knowing that our strength lies not in our individual abilities but in our collective determination to uphold each other.

Mark 10:8 (NASB) tells us, *"And the two shall become one flesh; so they are no longer two, but one flesh."*

This verse speaks of the transformative power of marriage, where two lives merge into one, creating a bond that is physical, emotional, and spiritual. Kathleen and I gained insight into this scripture through our shared journey, as we learned to let go of individualism and embrace unity.

God's concept of "one flesh" isn't limited to physical intimacy—it encompasses every aspect of a couple's relationship. It's about sharing hopes, dreams, and burdens. It's about blending two unique identities into a partnership where mutual respect and understanding thrive. For Kathleen and me, becoming one flesh meant acknowledging each other's differences while celebrating the ways they enrich our marriage.

This scripture also invites us to view marriage as a covenant—a sacred agreement that reflects God's love for His people. The merging of lives requires vulnerability, trust, and intentional effort to prioritize unity over division. It's not always easy; there are moments when selfishness threatens to undermine the bond. But Mark 10:8 reminds us that our calling as a couple is to pursue harmony, continually striving to reflect God's design for marriage.

One of the questions Kathleen and I often pondered was whether roles in a relationship could be interchangeable. Traditional views often assign rigid roles—men as providers and women as caretakers—but our experiences and faith have led us to a more flexible perspective.

While we believe that men should take on the role of spiritual leaders in the home, standing guard over their families and creating an atmosphere of faith, this does not mean women are excluded from leadership. Scripture shows us that God gifts talents and abilities to both men and women, enabling them to serve in various capacities. Throughout our marriage, Kathleen and I have found that our roles often shift based on the needs of the moment.

For instance, there have been seasons where Kathleen has taken the lead in areas such as managing our children's schedules or overseeing financial decisions, while I stepped into roles of emotional nurturing and support. These shifts didn't diminish our individual responsibilities; rather, they highlighted the beauty of teamwork and adaptability.

God calls each of us to use the gifts He has placed within us, regardless of gender. As Paul writes in Galatians 3:28 (NIV), *"There is neither male nor female, for you are all one in Christ Jesus."*

This reminds us that partnership is about complementing, not competing. Both men and women are capable of stepping into roles that serve the greater purpose of their union.

Merging two lives into one is no small task. Kathleen and I learned that achieving balance required intentionality and patience. We didn't always agree on every decision or approach, but we committed to seeking common ground, recognizing that our marriage was a team effort.

Finding neutral balance meant valuing each other's voices, even when they differed. We established boundaries to ensure that neither of us felt overpowered or undervalued. For example, we agreed to make major decisions together, respecting each other's opinions and working toward solutions that reflected unity.

Operating as a team also required humility—acknowledging when one of us needed help and being willing to step in for the other. For Kathleen and me, this looked like sharing responsibilities, supporting each other's dreams, and encouraging one another during moments of doubt. It also meant celebrating victories together, knowing that every success was the result of our collective effort.

Genesis 1:26–28 (ESV) reminds us of the equality inherent in God's creation: *"Let us make man in our image, after our likeness… male and female He created them."*

Kathleen and I often reflected on this verse, particularly when faced with cultural norms that sought to impose dominance or hierarchy in relationships.

God's original design did not give man dominion over woman—He gave them both dominion over creation. This truth challenges cultural and traditional views that place men above women, reinforcing the idea that partnership is meant to be equal and collaborative. Kathleen and I learned to set aside cultural expectations, focusing instead on what Scripture says about mutual respect and shared leadership.

As we navigated cultural differences in our marriage, we discovered the importance of honouring each other's perspectives without allowing traditions to overshadow our unity. By prioritizing God's design for partnership, we created a marriage rooted in equality, love, and mutual submission.

God equips both men and women with unique gifts and talents, empowering them to serve as leaders in their own right. Kathleen and I witnessed this truth in our marriage, where each of us contributed skills and abilities that strengthened our family. Kathleen's gift for nurturing relationships complemented my ability to lead with boldness, creating a balance that enriched our partnership.

Leadership, as we've learned, is not about authority; it's about service. Men are called to be spiritual leaders of their homes, standing guard and cultivating an atmosphere of faith. This role requires humility, accountability, and a commitment to modeling the fruits of the Spirit—love, joy, peace, patience, kindness, goodness, faithfulness, gentleness, and self-control (Galatians 5:22–23, NIV).

Women, too, are called to lead in ways that honour their God-given strengths. Kathleen has always exemplified wisdom, compassion, and discernment in her leadership, reminding me that her role in our marriage is just as vital as mine. Together, we strive to create a home where respect, collaboration, and love dominate.

Respect is the cornerstone of our marriage. Kathleen and I learned early on that honouring each other—both in public and private—was essential to maintaining trust and unity.

As a couple, we agreed to approach disagreements with discretion, avoiding public confrontations that could undermine our partnership. Kathleen has always been intentional about respecting me in public, ensuring that her actions reflect our teamwork and mutual support. Likewise, I've made it a priority to uplift her, celebrating her contributions and valuing her perspective.

Honour isn't just about outward gestures—it's about the heart. It's about seeing each other as God sees us, recognizing the unique worth and purpose in our roles. Kathleen and I have found that when we approach each other with respect, our marriage flourishes.

The scriptures that inspired Kathleen and me have shaped how we approach our marriage—as a partnership built on faith, love, and unity. Whether reflecting on Ecclesiastes 4:9–10, Mark 10:8, or Genesis 1:26–

28, we are reminded of God's design for relationships—a design that celebrates teamwork, equality, and mutual respect.

Through the years, we've learned to merge our lives, adapt our roles, and operate as a team. We've discovered the power of honouring each other's contributions, breaking cultural barriers, and leaning into God's calling for leadership. Most importantly, we've realized that success in marriage comes from standing together, embracing each other's strengths, and committing to the shared vision of building a kingdom that reflects God's love.

Kathleen and I continue to walk this journey with faith and determination, trusting that God will guide us as we strive to honour Him through our partnership. Together, as king and queen, we are building a legacy rooted in unity.

WHO IS MORE IMPORTANT?

The King or The Queen?

The question of importance between a king and a queen sparks a deeper conversation about equality, partnership, and shared purpose. Is one inherently more valuable than the other? Or is their true strength found in the way they work together? Kathleen and I have often reflected on this dynamic, especially when faced with moments that reveal our differences in personality, capabilities, and contributions to our marriage.

One story that sticks with me involves a mechanical problem in a car. The issue came down to two components: the battery, which cost $112, and the alternator's connector, which was just $19.99. To some, it may seem obvious—the battery is the more expensive part, so it must be more important. But the car wouldn't start without the connector. This simple truth shed light on our relationship and the roles Kathleen and I play as king and queen of our home. If I am the battery and Kathleen is the connector wire, who is more important? The answer is

WHO IS MORE IMPORTANT?

neither—both are essential. One cannot function properly without the other.

This revelation became a cornerstone for how we approach teamwork in our marriage. It taught us that the success of our partnership isn't about individual roles or what we can get from each other—it's about how we contribute to and complement one another. In this chapter, I'll explore what it means to honour both the king and queen in a relationship, emphasizing the value of teamwork, shared responsibility, and mutual respect. Through personal stories and relatable insights, we'll uncover how working together as equals builds a kingdom that thrives.

When people ask who is more important in a relationship—the king or the queen—they're often operating under the assumption that one role must be superior to the other. This mindset encourages comparison rather than collaboration, focusing on what each partner brings to the table rather than how they work together.

Kathleen and I have learned that this way of thinking can be harmful, especially in marriage. Early in our relationship, I sometimes felt pressure to "prove" my worth as the provider and protector. Kathleen, on the other hand, struggled with the fear that her quieter, introverted nature might make her contributions less visible. These insecurities were rooted in the misconception that one role must outweigh the other.

But life has shown us that importance is not about individual capabilities—it's about the synergy created when two people unite. The battery and connector wire analogy illustrates this beautifully. The car won't start without either component; their effectiveness depends on their interdependence. In the same way, a king and queen need each other to fulfill their shared purpose. Measuring importance doesn't strengthen a relationship—embracing partnership does.

One of the lessons Kathleen and I have learned is the importance of shifting our focus from "getting" to "giving." Early in marriage, it's easy to fall into the trap of wondering what your partner can do for you—how they can meet your needs, make you happy, or fill the gaps in your life. But true teamwork begins when both partners ask, "What can I contribute to our relationship?"

For me, this meant acknowledging that my role as the king wasn't just about leadership—it was about service. I realized that being the "head of the household" didn't mean dominating decisions or demanding respect. It meant leading with humility, listening to Kathleen's insights, and ensuring that her voice was heard in every aspect of our marriage.

Kathleen's perspective was equally transformative. She embraced her role as the queen, recognizing that her quiet strength and ability to nurture relationships were invaluable contributions to our kingdom. Together, we stopped focusing on what we could "get" from one another and began prioritizing how we could "give." This shift not only strengthened our bond but also created a culture of mutual respect and generosity.

Kathleen and I often reflect on how our differences have enriched our marriage. As a dominant, extroverted personality, I naturally gravitate toward leadership, decision-making, and action. Kathleen, on the other hand, brings introspection, patience, and emotional intelligence to our partnership. While these traits may seem opposite, they actually complement each other beautifully.

One example comes to mind from a particularly stressful season in our lives. We were faced with a financial challenge that required careful planning and decisive action. My initial response was to tackle the problem head-on, proposing bold solutions and pushing for immediate results. Kathleen, however, urged me to take a step back and consider all perspectives before making a decision. At first, I resisted, feeling that her cautious approach was slowing us down. But as we worked together,

WHO IS MORE IMPORTANT?

I realized that her patience brought clarity to the situation, allowing us to make choices that benefited our family in the long run.

This experience taught us that our strengths are not competing forces—they are complementary gifts. Kathleen's ability to ground me with wisdom and reflection enhances my decisiveness, while my enthusiasm and energy bring momentum to her thoughtful planning. Together, we create a balance that strengthens our marriage and builds a kingdom founded on trust, collaboration, and shared vision.

God's design for partnership emphasizes equality and shared responsibility. Kathleen and I have embraced this truth in our marriage, recognizing that both of us are called to lead, serve, and support one another.

Kathleen and I believe that teamwork is the lifeblood of a successful marriage. It's not about individual achievements—it's about collective effort. Just as a king and queen work together to govern their kingdom, couples must collaborate to build a life that reflects unity, purpose, and love.

One of the ways we cultivate teamwork is by respecting each other's strengths and limitations. Kathleen and I know that we each have areas where we excel and areas where we need support. By embracing this reality, we create an environment where both partners feel valued and empowered.

For instance, Kathleen's meticulous attention to detail often complements my big-picture thinking. When planning family events or tackling household projects, she ensures that every detail is accounted for, while I focus on the overall vision. This collaboration allows us to leverage our strengths while compensating for our weaknesses, proving that teamwork is greater than individual effort.

Another key aspect of teamwork in marriage is the commitment to serving the kingdom rather than pursuing personal gain. Kathleen and I often remind ourselves that our marriage is bigger than us—it's about creating a legacy for our family, serving our community, and reflecting God's love in the world.

This mindset encourages us to approach challenges with a spirit of selflessness. When disagreements arise, we prioritize what's best for our family and our relationship rather than focusing on who's right or wrong. By serving the kingdom together, we shift our focus from competition to collaboration, creating a partnership that thrives on mutual respect and shared purpose.

The question of importance between a king and a queen isn't about hierarchy—it's about partnership. Kathleen and I have learned that neither role is superior to the other; both are essential to building a kingdom that reflects unity, love, and purpose.

Like the battery and connector wire in a car, the king and queen rely on each other to function effectively. Their strength lies not in individual value but in the synergy created by their collaboration. Kathleen and I's journey has shown us that teamwork in marriage is not about comparing contributions—it's about celebrating them.

As king and queen of our home, we are committed to serving one another, honouring each other's strengths, and working together to build a life that reflects God's design for partnership. In doing so, we hope to inspire others to embrace the beauty of teamwork in their own relationships, proving that when couples unite, they can overcome any challenge and create a legacy that endures.

Teamwork is not just a principle—it's a way of life that transforms how we love, serve, and lead together. And as Kathleen and I continue to walk this path, we are reminded that the king and queen are always stronger together.

WHO IS MORE IMPORTANT?

ROLES AND RESPONSIBILITY

Identify What Your Can And Cannot Do

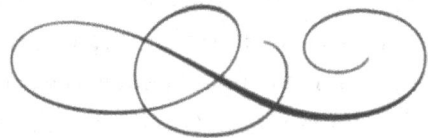

When Kathleen and I first married, we stepped into a journey filled with love, promise, and adventure. But like any journey, it also brought challenges that required us to learn and grow. With two distinct cultural and ethnic backgrounds, different personalities, and unique character traits, we had to figure out how to merge our strengths and weaknesses to function as a unit. It didn't take long to realize that working together would be our greatest asset. Raising seven children, managing a household, and maintaining our marriage demanded teamwork, understanding, and a willingness to adapt.

Kathleen and I have navigated the complexities of life together. By approaching our marriage as a partnership of equals—a king and queen—we discovered the beauty of complementing one another, compromising for the greater good, and learning to balance our roles. The process taught us that there is strength in vulnerability, power in collaboration, and blessings in honouring each other's unique contributions.

Coming from different cultural and ethnic backgrounds added an enriching dynamic to our relationship. Kathleen's upbringing was steeped in traditions that emphasized patience, empathy, and quiet strength. I, on the other hand, was raised in a more extroverted and assertive environment that valued decisiveness and action. These differences were evident in everything—from the way we communicated to the way we approached challenges.

Early in our marriage, I struggled to understand why Kathleen would take her time making decisions. Meanwhile, she found my quick, dominant approach overwhelming at times. It wasn't that either of us was wrong; we simply viewed the world through different lenses shaped by our backgrounds. Instead of allowing these differences to create a divide, we chose to see them as opportunities to learn from one another. Kathleen's thoughtful deliberation taught me the value of patience, while my assertiveness encouraged her to step into decisions with confidence.

Marriage, we discovered, is not about erasing differences but about weaving them into a tapestry that reflects unity. It's about recognizing that diversity brings richness and strength to the relationship. When we honoured each other's cultural and personal perspectives, we created a kingdom that was more inclusive, balanced, and resilient.

Research supports the idea that embracing cultural differences can strengthen relationships. According to Hatfield and Rapson (1993), couples who acknowledge and respect each other's unique backgrounds are better equipped to navigate conflicts and build lasting intimacy. For Kathleen and me, this meant actively seeking to understand one another's values and traditions, celebrating our differences, and finding common ground where our worlds overlapped.

One of the most humbling lessons I've learned in marriage is that I cannot do it all alone. As someone with a dominant personality, I initially thought it was my responsibility to shoulder the majority of the decisions, tasks, and challenges in our marriage. However, as life unfolded—especially with seven children to raise—I quickly realized that my strength alone was not enough. I needed Kathleen's partnership, her wisdom, and her unique strengths to keep our family thriving.

Collaboration became the cornerstone of our marriage. We learned to divide responsibilities based on our individual strengths. For example, I excelled at leading family discussions and making quick decisions during stressful situations, while Kathleen had a natural ability to connect with the children on an emotional level and create an atmosphere of peace in our home. Together, we formed a dynamic partnership where my strengths complemented her strengths, and our combined efforts created something far greater than what we could achieve alone.

What's more, I began to see the beauty in weaknesses—not just Kathleen's but my own. Where I lacked patience, she stepped in with understanding. Where she hesitated, I provided encouragement. Recognizing that our weaknesses could be opportunities for growth allowed us to approach each other with grace rather than criticism.

This idea is echoed in the concept of interdependence, which suggests that healthy relationships thrive when both partners contribute their unique strengths while leaning on each other's support (Knapp & Vangelisti, 2005). By embracing our interdependence, we found not only strength but also joy in working together.

Honour became a guiding principle in our marriage—a commitment to valuing each other's contributions, acknowledging each other's worth, and treating one another with respect. As a king and queen, we understood that the success of our "kingdom" depended on how we honoured each other's roles and responsibilities.

ROLES AND RESPONSIBILITY

For me, this meant respecting Kathleen's voice, even when her perspective differed from mine. It meant recognizing that her nurturing approach to parenting and her ability to create emotional stability were just as vital as my role as a provider and protector. Kathleen, in turn, honoured my leadership while offering insights and suggestions that enriched our decisions as a couple.

Honour also involved setting boundaries and limitations to ensure that neither of us felt overburdened or unappreciated. We learned to communicate openly about our needs, whether it was taking time to recharge individually or seeking help when we felt overwhelmed. By setting these boundaries, we created a space where both of us could thrive.

Trust, we found, was the foundation of honour. Trust allowed us to be vulnerable with each other, to share our fears and insecurities without judgment. It created an environment where we could collaborate freely, knowing that we had each other's backs. As Gottman and Silver (1999) highlight in their research, trust and respect are essential for building strong, lasting relationships. When partners feel honoured and valued, they are more likely to invest in the relationship and work together to overcome challenges.

No two people are the same, and that's especially true for Kathleen and me. Our differences in personality and character often led to disagreements, but we quickly learned that the key to harmony was not about "winning" but about complementing and compromising.

For example, I remember a time when we were deciding how to discipline one of our children who had made a poor choice. I believed in taking a firm approach, while Kathleen suggested a gentler, more understanding route. At first, I resisted her perspective, convinced that my way was the right way. But as we discussed it further, I realized that her approach brought a balance I hadn't considered. By listening to her insights and incorporating them into our plan, we were able to address the situation in a way that was both firm and compassionate.

Compromise, we discovered, is not about giving up but about meeting in the middle. It's about recognizing that both perspectives have value and finding a solution that honours both partners. This requires humility, patience, and a willingness to let go of pride for the sake of the relationship.

The art of complementing and compromising has been a continuous practice in our marriage. It has taught us to value each other's input, to approach disagreements with curiosity rather than defensiveness, and to prioritize the health of our relationship over individual preferences.

One of the most important lessons we've learned as a couple is the value of balance. Like a king and queen who share the responsibilities of ruling a kingdom, we recognized the need to support each other without overstepping boundaries. This meant defining our roles clearly while remaining flexible enough to adapt when needed.

For example, I took on the role of managing finances and making long-term plans for our family, while Kathleen excelled in creating daily routines and maintaining the emotional well-being of our children. These roles were not rigid but served as a framework that allowed us to function as a team.

Balancing each other also meant respecting our individual needs and limitations. There were times when I needed Kathleen to take the lead, especially during moments when I felt overwhelmed or uncertain. Similarly, there were times when she relied on me to step in and provide direction. By acknowledging our humanity and allowing each other the space to rest and recharge, we avoided burnout and resentment.

Setting boundaries was another critical aspect of balance. We agreed on what was acceptable in terms of communication, decision-making, and personal time. These boundaries created a sense of safety and mutual respect, allowing us to work together more effectively.

Through the years, Kathleen and I have come to see our marriage as a shared mission—a kingdom that we carry together. As king and queen, we understand that our individual roles are not about power or dominance but about serving each other and our family with love and humility.

Our journey has taught us that leadership in marriage is not about control; it's about collaboration. It's about recognizing that both partners bring unique strengths to the table and that those strengths are amplified when they work together. It's about honouring each other's contributions, embracing differences, and building a legacy of love and unity.

In the words of Keller and Keller (2011), "Marriage is a partnership, not a competition." This principle has been the guiding light in our relationship, reminding us that success is not measured by individual achievements but by the strength of our partnership.

As we continue to navigate life together, Kathleen and I remain committed to supporting each other, growing together, and carrying our "kingdom" forward. Whether it's raising our children, facing challenges, or celebrating milestones, we do it as a team—one that is stronger, wiser, and more united because of the lessons we've learned along the way.

The roles and responsibilities of a king and queen have always been fascinating, steeped in tradition, culture, and the unique dynamics of their partnership. Together, they form a powerful team that leads, nurtures, protects, and inspires. While their roles may differ, the beauty lies in how their responsibilities complement each other, creating harmony that sustains a thriving kingdom. Let's explore these timeless roles in warm, relatable language, focusing on the essence of their partnership, leadership, and shared commitment.

A king symbolizes strength and leadership. His role is often centered around protection, governance, and strategic decision-making for the kingdom's welfare. He is the pillar of authority, tasked with ensuring that the kingdom remains secure and prosperous. The king's responsibilities go beyond merely ruling; they extend to understanding the needs of his wife and children, cultivating alliances, and setting a vision for growth and stability.

One of the king's primary roles is as protector of his realm. He ensures the safety of the kingdom's borders, marshals forces in times of war, and makes difficult decisions to preserve peace. His responsibility is to maintain stability and act decisively when challenges arise.

Imagine the king as the shield of the kingdom, standing tall against external threats while nurturing internal unity. His decisions may require strength and resolve, but they are guided by the greater good of the family he serves.

A kingdom cannot flourish without direction. The king's role as a visionary leader allows him to set priorities for the kingdom's future. Whether fostering spiritual growth, cultural innovation by creating a blueprint for his children, the king ensures the kingdom remains a beacon of prosperity and hope.

Leadership is about inspiring others, and the king does this by embodying qualities like wisdom, courage, and determination. He is not just a ruler but a guide, charting a course that aligns with the kingdom's values and aspirations.

A king also serves as a judge, ensuring that "laws in his house" are upheld fairly and disputes are resolved with integrity. Justice is the foundation of any thriving community, and the king's role in maintaining it fosters trust and harmony among his family. By championing fairness, he sets an example for his children to follow, proving that power must be tempered with compassion and accountability.

ROLES AND RESPONSIBILITY

While the king's role comes with tremendous responsibility, his partnership with the queen is vital. Supporting her initiatives, valuing her insights, and working alongside her strengthens the unity that drives the kingdom. His leadership extends to being a loving partner, celebrating her contributions and empowering her to lead in her own right.

The queen's role, while distinct from the king's, is equally vital to the kingdom's success. She embodies compassion, diplomacy, and a nurturing spirit that enriches every aspect of the realm. The queen's responsibilities often focus on building relationships, championing causes, and fostering unity within the kingdom.

The queen serves as the heart of the kingdom, connecting with her husband and the children in ways that promote trust, loyalty, and hope. She is often seen as a figure of grace and empathy, reaching out to address the needs of the vulnerable, advocating for social progress, and ensuring that no one feels forgotten.

Her connection with her family bridges the gap between the throne and society. Whether comforting those in distress or celebrating achievements, the queen's presence reassures her husband and children that their voices matter.

While the king may focus on alliances from a strategic standpoint, the queen often excels in the art of diplomacy and relationship-building. Her ability to engage with other mothers and families brings mutual respect and cooperation. A queen's diplomacy enhances the kingdom's reputation, paving the way for lasting partnerships.

Imagine the queen as the "peacemaker" of the realm, whose warmth and influence bring stability even during challenging times. Her role in diplomacy demonstrates how compassion can complement power.

The queen often plays a significant role in preserving the kingdom's culture and traditions. Through celebrations, arts, and ceremonies, she nurtures the identity that unites the kingdom. Her leadership in these areas fosters pride and connection, reminding her family of the legacy they share.

Cultural preservation is a subtle yet powerful way to strengthen the kingdom. The queen's efforts in sustaining these traditions bring vibrancy to everyday life, ensuring that values and heritage remain central.

Just as the king supports the queen, she is equally instrumental in ensuring his success. Her wisdom, encouragement, and ability to see challenges from different perspectives enrich the king's decision-making. Their partnership thrives on mutual respect and collaboration, highlighting the importance of unity in leadership.

The queen's role as his confidante and ally ensures that the weight of leadership is shared, creating balance and strength in their shared journey.

A king and queen's ability to work together is what truly drives the kingdom forward. While their individual roles are distinct, their combined efforts create a foundation that sustains prosperity, peace, and progress. Their partnership is a beautiful example of shared leadership, rooted in love, respect, and understanding.

The king's authority and the queen's empathy complement one another, creating a leadership dynamic that is both firm and gentle. Decisions are made with wisdom and care, ensuring the well-being of the kingdom while fostering trust among the people.

This balance is a reminder that strength is not about dominance alone; it is about blending power with humanity to create lasting harmony.

Both the king and queen share an unwavering commitment to their kingdom. They lead not out of personal ambition but out of devotion to the people and the legacy they uphold. Their roles remind us that true

ROLES AND RESPONSIBILITY

leadership is about service—about uplifting others and working toward the common good.

CHARACTER AND PERSONALITIES

Strength Comes With Unity

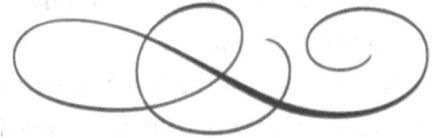

Kathleen and I have always recognized that we are different—not just in our habits and preferences, but in the very essence of our personalities. Like any couple, like a king and queen, we've had to learn to appreciate those differences rather than let them divide us. A kingdom cannot stand if its rulers are constantly at odds, struggling for control instead of working in harmony. Over the years, we've come to understand that strength comes through unity, and embracing our unique qualities has helped us build a marriage that is balanced, resilient, and deeply connected.

A kingdom flourishes when its leaders learn to work together, complementing each other's strengths and compensating for each other's weaknesses. Kathleen has taught me patience, and I've helped her embrace moments of spontaneity. She sees things that I might

CHARACTER AND PERSONALITIES

overlook, and I provide direction when things feel uncertain. Instead of competing, we blend our strengths to protect what we've built—our marriage, our family, and our shared future.

Just as kings and queens throughout history have had different temperaments, leadership styles, and perspectives, yet ruled with a common goal, Kathleen and I strive to lead our relationship in the same way. Our unity makes us stronger, and by appreciating the unique qualities we bring into our marriage, we have fortified the love, trust, and resilience that allow us to stand together—not just as husband and wife, but as partners committed to ruling our kingdom with wisdom and grace.

Marriage is the union of two individuals, each with their unique personalities and characters shaped by their upbringing, life experiences, and personal values. It's no wonder that when two people come together, differences arise. These differences, however, are not obstacles—they are opportunities to learn, grow, and deepen the bond between partners. Kathleen and I have lived this reality throughout our marriage. Like all couples, we've had to navigate the interplay of our personalities and characters. While our differences initially seemed like points of tension, we eventually learned to adjust and accept them as strengths that could enrich our relationship.

This journey of understanding and appreciating each other's personalities has taught us valuable lessons about love, respect, and adaptability. It is not about trying to change one another—it is about celebrating who we are and learning to work together in harmony. In this chapter, I'll share insights from our lived experiences, highlighting how Kathleen and I learned to embrace our differences and find balance in our partnership.

Kathleen and I often reflect on how much our upbringing influenced the personalities we brought into our marriage. She grew up in a nurturing household where emotions were freely expressed, and communication was centered around connection and understanding. This environment shaped her into a compassionate and empathetic person who values emotional intimacy and cares deeply for others.

I, on the other hand, was raised in an environment that emphasized practicality, discipline, and resilience. My upbringing encouraged a focus on logic and problem-solving, shaping me into someone who prioritizes goals, efficiency, and structure. While these traits served me well in many aspects of life, they often led me to approach situations with a more rigid mindset, making it harder to embrace flexibility and emotional expression.

When Kathleen and I first married, these differences became apparent in the way we handled conflicts, made decisions, and communicated with one another. Kathleen's emotional nature sometimes clashed with my rational approach, leading to misunderstandings and frustration. For example, when faced with challenges, she would want to talk through her feelings, while I preferred to "fix" the problem and move on. These contrasting styles often left us feeling disconnected, wondering how we could bridge the gap.

Research supports the idea that upbringing and life experiences shape personality and behaviour in relationships. According to Roberts et al. (2020), personality traits are influenced by early childhood experiences, cultural norms, and social interactions, which in turn affect how individuals approach intimacy and conflict. Understanding these factors can help couples empathize with each other's perspectives and work toward greater harmony.

One of the most important lessons Kathleen and I learned was the value of adjustment—not to change who we were, but to better meet each other's needs. Marriage, we discovered, is about making room for your partner's personality without losing your own.

For instance, Kathleen's emotional nature often required a level of patience and understanding that didn't come naturally to me. In the early days of our marriage, I struggled to empathize when she expressed feelings that seemed irrational to me. But as I listened more intentionally and sought to understand the emotions behind her words, I began to appreciate the depth of her perspective. Kathleen's emotional insights often highlighted aspects of a situation I hadn't considered, helping me approach decisions with greater sensitivity.

Kathleen, in turn, had to adjust to my rational nature, particularly when it came to decision-making. She learned that my focus on logic and structure wasn't dismissive of her emotions—it was a way of ensuring stability and consistency for our family. By embracing this aspect of my personality, Kathleen found ways to integrate her emotional insights into practical solutions, creating a balance that worked for both of us.

Adjustment is not about losing your identity—it's about expanding it to include your partner's needs and perspectives. Couples who learn to adjust create a partnership that is adaptable and resilient, capable of navigating the complexities of life together.

One of the turning points in our marriage came when Kathleen and I shifted our mindset from seeing our differences as challenges to viewing them as strengths. Instead of trying to make each other conform to a single way of being, we began to celebrate the unique qualities we brought to the relationship.

Kathleen's ability to connect emotionally has been one of the greatest blessings in our marriage. She has a gift for nurturing relationships, creating an atmosphere of warmth and understanding in our home. Her empathy allows her to see beyond surface-level issues, addressing the heart of what truly matters.

My rational nature, on the other hand, provides structure and clarity. I excel at planning, organizing, and ensuring that our goals align with our values. While Kathleen's emotional intelligence brings connection, my logical approach ensures stability and direction. Together, these qualities complement one another, creating a partnership that thrives on diversity.

Celebrating differences is a practice rooted in appreciation and respect. When couples embrace the unique qualities of their partner, they build a relationship that values individuality while fostering connection.

Differences in personality can sometimes lead to conflict, but Kathleen and I have learned that conflict is not the enemy—it is an opportunity for growth. When handled with care and respect, disagreements can deepen understanding and strengthen the relationship.

Early in our marriage, conflicts often arose from misunderstandings about our communication styles. Kathleen's emotional expression sometimes felt overwhelming to me, while my logical approach made her feel unheard. These moments of tension required us to step back, reflect, and find ways to bridge the gap.

One strategy we've adopted is focusing on the issue at hand rather than assigning blame. For example, if Kathleen feels frustrated about a decision, I make an effort to validate her emotions before presenting my perspective. Similarly, she listens to my rationale with curiosity rather than defensiveness. This approach creates a safe space for dialogue, allowing us to address the conflict without damaging our connection.

Couples who navigate conflict effectively often demonstrate emotional intelligence and communication skills that foster collaboration. According to Gottman and Silver (2019), successful conflict resolution involves understanding each partner's needs, expressing empathy, and working together to find solutions. Kathleen and I have found that these principles are key to maintaining harmony in our relationship.

CHARACTER AND PERSONALITIES

One of the most transformative lessons Kathleen and I have learned is the importance of acceptance. In marriage, it's easy to focus on what you wish your partner would do differently or how they could change to better meet your expectations. But true love is rooted in appreciation—seeing your partner for who they are and valuing them as God's creation.

For Kathleen and me, this meant embracing our personalities without judgment. I've come to cherish Kathleen's emotional intelligence, seeing it as a source of connection and compassion that enriches our relationship. Kathleen, in turn, has learned to appreciate my rational nature, recognizing it as a strength that provides stability and direction.

Acceptance also involves letting go of unrealistic expectations. Kathleen and I have stopped trying to "fix" each other, focusing instead on how we can support and encourage each other's growth. This shift has created a culture of love and respect in our marriage, allowing both of us to thrive as individuals and as partners.

Lessons for Couples: Building a Relationship That Celebrates Differences

Through our journey, Kathleen and I have learned several lessons that can help other couples navigate differences in personality and character:

1. **Understand Each Other's Backgrounds:** Recognize how upbringing and life experiences shape personality traits. This understanding fosters empathy and provides context for your partner's behaviour.
2. **Adjust Without Losing Yourself:** Find ways to meet your partner's needs while maintaining your identity. Adjustment is about creating space for both personalities to thrive.

3. **Celebrate Differences:** View your partner's unique qualities as strengths that enrich the relationship. Embrace diversity as a source of balance and harmony.
4. **Navigate Conflict with Respect:** Approach disagreements with curiosity and empathy. Focus on resolving the issue rather than assigning blame.
5. **Practice Acceptance:** Love your partner for who they are, valuing their individuality as a gift. Let go of unrealistic expectations and focus on supporting their growth.

Kathleen and I's journey of appreciating our personalities and characters has been one of discovery, growth, and love. While our differences initially seemed like challenges, they have become the strengths that define our relationship. By adjusting to fit each other's needs, celebrating our unique qualities, and practicing acceptance, we have built a partnership that thrives on respect and harmony.

Our marriage is a testament to the idea that diversity in personality is not a barrier—it is a blessing. When couples learn to navigate their differences with grace and understanding, they create a relationship that reflects the beauty of God's design for unity. Kathleen and I continue to cherish the journey of embracing who we are, knowing that our partnership is stronger because of it.

CHARACTER AND PERSONALITIES

EMBRACING DIFFERENCES

Introvert and Extrovert

A king and queen must learn to embrace their differences, recognizing that ruling a kingdom requires a balance of strengths. Just as Kathleen and I had to understand how our personalities shaped our marriage, we saw that being an extrovert or an introvert could either strengthen or challenge our dynamic—depending on how we approached it. I am naturally outgoing, the "dancing monkey" who thrives on energy and interaction, while Kathleen leans toward quiet reflection and deep thought.

Early on, we noticed how these differences influenced the way we communicated, solved problems, and even spent time together. One day, I playfully asked Kathleen when we go to heaven, she would want to be with the introverts or the extroverts. Without hesitation, she said, *"I don't want to be with the introverts—it would be too boring!"* We laughed at the idea because I had never imagined an introvert in that way. She explained that while she appreciates deep thought and quiet moments, she truly loves the boldness, excitement, and energy that I bring into our lives. That moment reminded us how much we need each other's differences, and that rather than seeing them as obstacles, we must embrace them as the very qualities that make our relationship whole.

When Kathleen and I first married, one thing quickly became apparent—we were complete opposites when it came to personality traits. Kathleen was deeply introverted, finding joy in quiet moments, reflective solitude, and intimate conversations. On the other hand, I was the quintessential extrovert—always energized by social gatherings, vibrant discussions, and the buzz of activity. At first, our differences seemed like mountains to climb. How could two people at opposite ends of the personality pendulum build a life together?

What we learned over time was a lesson that transformed our marriage: differences are not barriers; they are bridges. Being opposite in personality didn't make us incompatible—it made us complementary. Kathleen's introversion taught me the value of slowing down, while my extroversion brought her out of her shell in ways that enriched her life. Together, we discovered that the positives of introversion and extroversion are worth celebrating, and that diversity in personality is a gift to cherish, not a challenge to overcome.

Through personal experiences and relatable examples, Kathleen and I learned to appreciate our differences, focusing on the positives, and building a marriage rooted in mutual respect and understanding. Along the way, we have explored the latest insights into personality psychology and offer practical advice for navigating the complexities of introvert-extrovert partnerships.

Kathleen's introversion was evident in her calm demeanour and preference for solitude. She thrived in environments where she could reflect, recharge, and connect deeply with herself and a few trusted individuals. As someone who finds comfort in quiet spaces, Kathleen often needed time to process her thoughts before sharing them, and she valued meaningful conversations over small talk.

On the other hand, my extroversion was the polar opposite. I drew energy from interactions with people and thrived in social settings. My personality leaned toward spontaneity, external processing of thoughts, and a love for dynamic, fast-paced environments. For me, silence was rarely comfortable—I preferred to talk through challenges, brainstorm ideas aloud, and share my excitement with others.

Recognizing that introversion and extroversion exist on a spectrum helped us understand each other better. Introverts are not necessarily shy, nor are extroverts always outgoing—it's about where we find our energy. Introverts recharge in quiet, low-stimulation environments, while extroverts gain energy from engaging with the world around them (Cain, 2012). Kathleen and I were two unique individuals operating on different frequencies, but we learned that these frequencies could harmonize beautifully.

One of the most transformative moments in our marriage came when we decided to write down the positives of our personality traits—both introvert and extrovert. This simple exercise reminded us that we each brought unique strengths to the relationship, and by focusing on those strengths, we could build a life that honoured both perspectives.

Kathleen's introversion was a gift in so many ways. She had a natural ability to listen deeply, empathize with others, and think through challenges with careful deliberation. Her calm presence created a sense of stability in our home, and her attention to detail ensured that nothing went unnoticed. Kathleen's introspection enriched our conversations, bringing depth and insight to even the smallest topics.

As an extrovert, I contributed strengths of my own. My enthusiasm and energy created momentum in our marriage, encouraging us to take risks, try new things, and explore the world with curiosity. I excelled at connecting with people, building networks, and fostering a sense of community. My outgoing nature helped us stay socially active, introducing Kathleen to experiences and friendships that brought joy to her life.

Together, we realized that introversion and extroversion were not opposites—they were complements. Kathleen's grounded presence balanced my energetic spirit, creating a partnership that was both dynamic and steady. By celebrating the positives of our personalities, we found harmony in our differences.

Despite the beauty of our complementary traits, there were moments when our differences led to friction. Kathleen often felt drained by my need for social interaction, while I struggled to understand her desire for quiet reflection. There were times when I wanted to host gatherings at home, but Kathleen longed for an evening of solitude.

What helped us navigate these challenges was the willingness to communicate openly and respect each other's needs. Kathleen and I learned that compromise was key—sometimes we prioritized her need for quiet, and other times we embraced my love for connection. The goal was not to erase our differences but to create space for both personalities to thrive.

Research supports the idea that introvert-extrovert relationships can be enriching but require intentional effort. According to Helgoe (2020), couples with differing personality traits are more likely to experience misunderstandings but can achieve greater balance when they embrace their differences as strengths. This insight encouraged us to approach our differences with curiosity, not judgment, allowing friction to become an opportunity for growth.

One of the most important lessons Kathleen and I learned was the value of appreciating personality diversity. Trying to change each other or fit into the same mould would have diminished the beauty of our partnership. Instead, we chose to honour our individuality, recognizing that our differences were what made our marriage unique.

Kathleen's introversion taught me the value of slowing down and appreciating the quiet moments in life. I began to see the beauty in her thoughtful approach to decision-making and her ability to connect deeply with others. She helped me understand the importance of listening—not just hearing words but truly understanding the emotions behind them.

In turn, my extroversion brought Kathleen out of her shell in ways that enriched her life. She began to enjoy social gatherings, discovering the joy of building connections with people. My enthusiasm encouraged her to take risks and explore new experiences, fostering growth and adventure in her life.

Our journey has been a testament to the idea that different is good. Trying to make Kathleen more extroverted or myself more introverted would have stifled our natural gifts. Instead, we learned to celebrate our individuality and use our strengths to build a partnership that reflected both perspectives.

Building a life together required Kathleen and me to merge our personalities and find balance. One of the strategies we employed was setting boundaries to ensure that neither of us felt overwhelmed. For example, we agreed to alternate between social events and quiet evenings, allowing Kathleen time to recharge while giving me the interaction I craved.

We also learned the importance of dividing responsibilities based on our strengths. Kathleen's attention to detail made her excellent at planning and organizing, while my outgoing nature made me well-suited for networking and engaging with others. By embracing these roles, we created a dynamic partnership that leveraged the best of both worlds.

Operating as a team also meant respecting each other's differences. Kathleen and I committed to listening without judgment, valuing each other's perspectives, and approaching challenges as a united front. This sense of teamwork helped us navigate the complexities of marriage while fostering mutual respect and understanding.

Throughout our journey, Kathleen and I have made mistakes, taken missteps, and faced moments of frustration. But what has sustained our marriage is the practice of forgiveness and grace. We've learned that no one is perfect—we all make bad decisions and wrong choices, but these moments don't define us.

Forgiveness has allowed us to move past misunderstandings and focus on building a stronger relationship. Grace has reminded us to approach each other with kindness, even when tensions arise. Kathleen and I have come to see challenges not as failures but as opportunities to grow and learn together.

Kathleen and I's journey as an introvert-extrovert couple has been one of growth, discovery, and celebration. We've learned to embrace our differences, focus on the positives, and honour each other's individuality. Our partnership is a testament to the idea that personality diversity is a gift—a source of strength, balance, and enrichment.

The lessons we've learned are ones that extend beyond marriage. Appreciating personality diversity is essential in all relationships, whether romantic, professional, or familial. By focusing on strengths, communicating openly, and practicing forgiveness, we can build connections that celebrate individuality while fostering unity.

Kathleen and I continue to thrive as a team, committed to honouring our differences and working together to build a life rooted in love and understanding. The introvert-extrovert dynamic may have started as a challenge, but it has become one of the greatest gifts in our marriage—a reminder that opposites truly can attract and thrive.

EMBRACE A TEAM MINDSET

Building Together for Success

A *king and queen* must learn to embrace a team mindset, recognizing that success is never built alone—it is forged through unity, understanding, and shared purpose. Throughout history, we see examples of kings and queens ruling side by side, each bringing unique strengths to their leadership. They knew that the kingdom's survival depended on their ability to work together, not against each other.

Kathleen and I have learned that the same principle applies to marriage—when we focus on teamwork rather than individual victories, our relationship flourishes. It is not about who leads and who follows, but about walking together, facing life's challenges as partners, and making decisions that strengthen our family. There were times when we struggled, when differing opinions pulled us in opposite directions, but the moment we embraced the mindset of building together, everything changed. Our marriage became stronger, our love deeper, and our

EMBRACE A TEAM MINDSET

family healthier because we ruled as one, not two individuals competing for control. True success in marriage comes from realizing that you are not fighting each other—you are fighting for each other.

Having a team mindset isn't just about working with others—it's about embracing collaboration, sharing a vision, and moving forward as a unified force. Whether in marriage, work, friendships, or community settings, a team mindset transforms how individuals approach challenges, celebrate victories, and nurture relationships. It focuses on collective strengths, mutual respect, and the belief that the group's success outweighs any individual's accomplishments.

Kathleen and I have learned that a team mindset through the lens of real-life experiences, uncovered the principles that make teamwork thrive. We carry a mindset that enhances relationships and reflect on practical applications in various areas of life. Drawing on warm, relatable stories and the latest research, we emphasize the power of building together and succeeding together.

Every successful team starts with a shared vision—a common purpose that unites individuals and gives them direction. When I reflect on my own experiences, I realize how transformative it was to align with Kathleen and the children around a shared goal. Whether it was raising a family with Kathleen, collaborating with colleagues at work, or building community initiatives, having a clear vision provided the clarity and focus needed to move forward as one.

For example, when Kathleen and I began our journey as parents, we quickly realized that raising seven children would require more than individual effort—it would demand teamwork. Our shared vision was simple yet profound: to create a loving, supportive environment where our children could thrive. This vision guided every decision we made, from establishing routines to navigating challenges. It reminded us that our roles as partners and parents were interconnected, and success would only come if we worked together as a team.

A shared vision doesn't mean uniformity—it means unity. According to DeChurch and Mesmer-Magnus (2010), teams are most effective when they align around a clear, shared goal while allowing room for individual contributions. A shared vision creates synergy, fostering collaboration and ensuring that every team member feels valued for their unique input.

One of the most important aspects of a team mindset is prioritizing collaboration over competition. In a world that often emphasizes individual achievement, it's easy to fall into the trap of competing with those around us. But true teamwork thrives when individuals set aside their personal agendas and focus on what's best for the group.

I remember a moment early in my career when a colleague and I were tasked with presenting a major project to leadership. At first, I was tempted to push my ideas to the forefront, eager to demonstrate my capabilities. However, as we began working together, I realized that my colleague's perspective brought depth and clarity to our presentation. By collaborating rather than competing, we created a proposal that was far stronger than anything either of us could have produced alone.

Kathleen and I have applied the same principle in our marriage. We've learned that success doesn't come from trying to "outshine" one another—it comes from building each other up, celebrating each other's strengths, and working together toward shared goals. Collaboration fosters trust and unity, reminding us that the journey is as important as the destination.

Recent research emphasizes the value of collaboration in fostering team effectiveness. Braun et al. (2018) found that cooperative behaviours, including open communication and mutual support, enhance team performance and strengthen interpersonal relationships. These behaviours create an environment where individuals feel safe to share ideas, take risks, and support one another without fear of judgment or rivalry.

EMBRACE A TEAM MINDSET

A team mindset isn't about erasing individuality—it's about honouring the unique contributions of each member. When individuals bring their diverse skills, perspectives, and experiences to the table, the team benefits from a richer, more dynamic approach to challenges.

Kathleen and I embody this principle in our partnership. While we approach life differently—she's thoughtful and deliberate, while I'm action-oriented and assertive—we've come to appreciate how these differences enhance our decision-making and problem-solving. For instance, when faced with a financial challenge, Kathleen's cautious planning ensures stability, while my decisiveness helps us move forward quickly. Together, our combined strengths create balance and resilience.

Respecting individual contributions requires humility, a willingness to listen, and a commitment to valuing others' voices. It's about recognizing that no one person has all the answers, and success comes from leveraging the collective wisdom of the group. Teams that embrace diversity are more innovative and adaptable, capable of tackling complex challenges with creativity and insight (Van Knippenberg et al., 2020).

Life is full of challenges, and a team mindset transforms how individuals approach them. Instead of facing obstacles alone, teams rally together, supporting one another and finding solutions as a collective. The strength of a team lies in its ability to turn adversity into opportunity, drawing on shared resources and resilience.

One of the most challenging seasons for Kathleen and me came when we were raising our seven children while managing demanding careers. Between financial pressures, conflicting schedules, and the everyday demands of parenting, we often felt overwhelmed. But rather than allowing these challenges to create distance between us, we chose to face them together.

Kathleen's unwavering encouragement reminded me that I didn't have to carry the weight alone, while my optimism and determination gave her the confidence to keep moving forward. By supporting each other, we found creative solutions to our challenges—whether it was dividing responsibilities, seeking help from extended family, or simplifying our routines. This season taught us the power of teamwork and reinforced the belief that together, we could overcome anything.

Teams that navigate challenges effectively demonstrate resilience, adaptability, and emotional intelligence. According to Edmondson (2019), psychological safety—an environment where individuals feel secure to express themselves without fear of negative consequences—plays a key role in how teams respond to adversity. Building psychological safety fosters trust, enabling team members to collaborate and support one another during difficult times.

A team mindset isn't just about working through challenges—it's about celebrating victories. Recognizing and honouring shared accomplishments reinforces the bond between team members, reminding them of the value of their collaboration.

In our marriage, Kathleen and I have learned the importance of celebrating even the smallest milestones. Whether it's achieving a financial goal, navigating a tough parenting situation, or simply making it through a stressful week, we take time to acknowledge our progress and express gratitude for each other's efforts.

Celebrating success together fosters positivity and strengthens relationships. Research by Fredrickson (2013) highlights the role of positive emotions in building resilience and enhancing group dynamics. When teams take time to celebrate their achievements, they create a culture of encouragement and gratitude, which fuels motivation and deepens connection.

A team mindset isn't confined to any specific area of life—it's a principle that applies to every relationship and endeavor. From workplaces to families, friendships to community initiatives, adopting a team mindset creates unity and drives success.

In my own life, I've found that living with a team mindset requires intentional effort. It means showing up for others, listening with empathy, and valuing their perspectives. It means setting aside ego and embracing the belief that collaboration is the key to growth. Most importantly, it means recognizing that success isn't measured by individual accomplishments but by the collective impact of the team.

Kathleen and I strive to embody these principles in our marriage, our parenting, and our community involvement. We've learned that the team mindset isn't just an approach—it's a way of life that transforms how we connect, build, and thrive together.

To have a team mindset is to embrace the power of collaboration, respect, and shared vision. It's about recognizing that we are stronger together than we are alone, and that success comes from lifting each other up and working toward common goals. Whether in personal relationships, professional settings, or community endeavours, the team mindset creates a foundation of trust, unity, and resilience.

Kathleen and I have experienced the beauty of this mindset firsthand—through the challenges we've overcome, the victories we've celebrated, and the lessons we've learned along the way. By embracing the team mindset, we've created a partnership that thrives on mutual support, encouragement, and respect. And the impact of this approach extends far beyond our marriage—it shapes how we interact with others, approach life's challenges, and build a legacy of love and unity.

The team mindset is a reminder that we are never alone—that when we work together, we can achieve extraordinary things.

UNITY IN LEADERSHIP

Rule Together As A Team

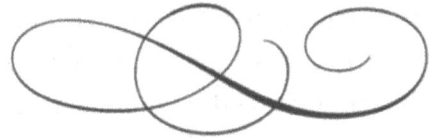

The king and queen's ability to unite in leadership demonstrates the power of teamwork. Their collaboration showcases the importance of shared responsibility, highlighting how different strengths can come together to achieve greatness. This unity inspires their children to work together, fostering a sense of community and purpose.

The roles of a king and queen may have historical significance, but they also provide valuable lessons for modern relationships. At their core, these roles symbolize partnership, mutual respect, and the importance of working together to overcome challenges.

In any relationship—whether romantic, familial, or professional—these principles remain relevant. The king and queen's dynamic reminds us that:

- **Balance matters:** Each partner brings unique strengths to the table, and honouring those differences creates harmony.
- **Support is vital:** Encouragement and respect strengthen the bond between partners, empowering them to face challenges together.
- **Shared vision drives success:** Having a common goal ensures unity and fosters growth.

The essence of the king and queen's partnership reminds us that great relationships are built on love, trust, and collaboration. It's a beautiful reflection of how two individuals, united in purpose, can achieve extraordinary things.

The roles and responsibilities of a king and queen are deeply intertwined, showcasing the beauty of shared leadership. While their individual tasks may differ, their unity is what allows the kingdom to flourish. The king's strength and vision, paired with the queen's compassion and grace, create a foundation of harmony, resilience, and progress.

Their partnership is not just about ruling; it's about serving their people, preserving their heritage, and inspiring others to live with purpose. By working together, they carry the kingdom forward, proving that true leadership is rooted in love, respect, and collaboration.

In the end, the story of a king and queen is more than a tale of power—it's a celebration of partnership, resilience, and the timeless pursuit of a better future. Their legacy teaches us that together, we can overcome challenges and build something extraordinary, one step at a time.

Kathleen and I have been through it all—life's storms and sunshine, triumphs and challenges, heartbreaks and celebrations. Standing with each other through thick and thin has been more than just a commitment;

it's been the foundation of our marriage, the glue that keeps us strong, the promise that no matter what comes our way, we're in this together.

When we said our vows, we weren't just agreeing to love one another in the good times—we were promising to be each other's refuge when the road became tough. Life, as we've learned, has its fair share of battles, but it's in those battles that our bond has grown stronger, our partnership has deepened, and our love has proved its endurance. We learned early on that protecting each other, our home, and what we hold dear wasn't just about facing external challenges—it was about standing guard over our hearts, our trust, and the world we've built together.

Kathleen has always been my hero. She may not wear a cape, but her quiet strength, fierce loyalty, and unwavering belief in me have carried me through more difficult days than I can count. While I have a more dominant personality—loud, outgoing, and ready to tackle the world—Kathleen grounds me with her calm presence and gentle wisdom. In many ways, she balances my fire with her steady grace, reminding me that true strength isn't always loud—it's often found in quiet determination and selfless love.

One evening, amidst one of life's tougher seasons, Kathleen said something to me that changed my world forever. We were sitting in our car on our way home, worn out from the challenges we were facing, feeling the weight of financial stress, parenting responsibilities, and the uncertainties of our future. I confessed to her that I felt like I was failing—not as a husband, not as a father, but as a man. I told her I didn't know how much longer I could carry the burden, how much longer I could fight.

She looked at me with all the compassion in her heart, her eyes steady and full of love, and said five words that would forever be etched in my memory: *"I will fight for you."*

Those words shattered the fear and doubt I was holding. Until that moment, I thought it was my job to fight for her, for our family, for our marriage. But her declaration reminded me that I wasn't alone in this battle—we were partners, standing shoulder to shoulder, facing life together. Kathleen's promise to fight for me gave me the courage to keep going, the strength to rise above the struggles, and the reassurance that I didn't have to carry the weight alone.

It's moments like these that teach us what love really looks like. Love isn't just about saying "I'm here for you"—it's about showing up every day, even when it's hard, even when it's inconvenient, even when you don't have all the answers. Kathleen's words were a promise to me that our marriage wasn't a one-sided effort, but a shared commitment built on trust, respect, and determination to protect what we had created together.

Over the years, we've fought many battles together—not just external challenges, but the inner struggles that every couple faces. We've had disagreements, we've stumbled over misunderstandings, and we've learned hard lessons about patience, humility, and grace. But through it all, we've remained each other's supporters, best friends, lovers, and more.

Kathleen is my hero because she fights for what matters. She fights fiercely for our children, making sure they grow up knowing they are deeply loved, cherished, and valued. She instills in them a strong foundation of faith, ensuring they are grounded in their relationship with God and committed to serving Him. Since I was often at work during the early mornings, I encouraged her to lead devotions before school, praying with them and setting a spiritual tone for the day. For our family, going to church wasn't just an option—it was an essential part of our lives. I had firmly declared, "As for me and my house, we will serve the Lord," and together, we embraced that calling wholeheartedly.

We fight for our family by prioritizing time together, creating memories that bond us and remind us of the joy in life. We fight for our dreams by encouraging each other to pursue what makes us happy, supporting each other's goals, and celebrating each other's achievements. And we fight for our marriage by choosing love every day—not just in words, but in actions that demonstrate our commitment to one another.

She fights for our marriage, reminding me that every challenge is an opportunity to grow closer and stronger together. And she fights for me—not just as her husband but as a man she believes in, respects, and loves deeply.

I'd like to think that I'm her hero too. I fight for her by standing beside her, by listening to her dreams and fears, by celebrating her victories and comforting her in her losses. I fight for her by protecting her heart, ensuring she knows that she is seen, heard, and valued. Together, we've learned that being each other's heroes isn't about grand gestures or extraordinary feats—it's about the everyday choices we make to love, support, and honour each other.

Our marriage is like a castle—a strong, unshakable fortress that we've built brick by brick. But like any castle, it needs protecting. Life has tried to storm the gates, but Kathleen and I have stood guard, defending what we've built with determination and grace. The walls of our castle are reinforced by communication, respect, and forgiveness—the pillars that hold us up when life tries to tear us down.

Being each other's heroes means standing in the gap for one another when life feels overwhelming. It means seeing the best in each other, even on our worst days. It means lifting each other up when the weight of the world feels too heavy to carry alone. Kathleen has done this for me time and time again, and I hope she feels the same about me.

As I reflect on our journey, I am reminded of the power of partnership—the power of two people coming together to create something extraordinary. Kathleen's words, "I will fight for you," encapsulate everything our marriage stands for: unity, resilience, and an unwavering belief in the strength of love.

And so, we continue to fight. We fight not against each other but alongside each other. We protect what is sacred—our hearts, our family, our dreams. We remind each other that love is not a fleeting feeling but a daily choice to stand together in the face of life's challenges.

Kathleen and I are each other's heroes, supporters, best friends, lovers, and so much more. And every day, we choose to carry our castle forward, brick by brick, with love as our foundation and trust as our guide. Life will continue to test us, but as long as we have each other, we will stand strong—together, as king and queen, fighting for the kingdom we've built and the love that sustains us.

If there's one thing our story teaches, it's that love is worth fighting for. And when both partners are committed to protecting and nurturing their relationship, there's nothing they can't overcome. Kathleen's promise to fight for me changed my world, and together, we are changing ours—building a legacy of love that will stand the test of time.

ACCOUNTABILITY

A Cornerstone for Trust and Growth

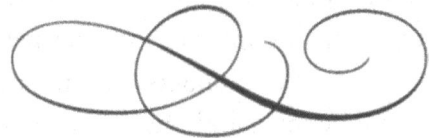

A *king and queen* must embrace accountability, recognizing it as the cornerstone of trust and growth in their relationship. Throughout history, rulers who thrived did so not by acting independently, but by remaining accountable to each other, ensuring their kingdom remained strong and unified. Kathleen and I have learned this same lesson in marriage—our bond is strengthened when we take responsibility for our actions, decisions, and the way we nurture our relationship.

Over the years, we have faced moments where our—children, family, or friends—could have created division between us or "splitting." But by standing firm in our commitment to accountability, we ensured that no outside influence could weaken our unity.

Marriage is about owning our roles, communicating openly, and remaining honest with one another—never shifting blame, but always working together to resolve challenges. When a king and queen stand accountable to each other, their kingdom flourishes, and for us, that kingdom is our marriage, our family, and the life we have built together.

In relationships, accountability serves as a cornerstone of trust, growth, and emotional safety. While love is often the initial spark that brings two people together, it is accountability that helps maintain the strength and integrity of their union. Accountability isn't just about acknowledging mistakes or being transparent—it's about creating a space where trust can flourish, where weaknesses can be addressed without shame, and where mutual support reinforces the foundation of the relationship.

Kathleen and I have learned over the years that accountability is essential for building a thriving partnership. Like most couples, we've had moments when egos got in the way or when it was easier to avoid a difficult conversation than to confront an issue head-on. But through these experiences, we've come to understand that accountability is not a burden—it's a gift that deepens intimacy, strengthens trust, and helps couples navigate the challenges that life inevitably brings.

Accountability in a relationship is the practice of being honest, transparent, and responsible for your actions, decisions, and emotions. It requires individuals to acknowledge their mistakes, communicate openly, and work together to find solutions. At its core, accountability is about honouring the commitment you've made to your partner and to the relationship itself.

For Kathleen and me, accountability has meant creating a relationship where there are no secrets, no locked doors, and no hidden corners. This doesn't mean that we don't value privacy—every individual needs personal space—but it does mean that we strive to live in a way that invites trust rather than suspicion. Whether it's sharing access to our phones, laptops, or social media accounts, we've chosen to prioritize transparency as a way of fostering trust and intimacy.

Accountability also means being willing to address difficult topics rather than sweeping them under the rug. In the early years of our marriage, there were moments when I avoided certain conversations because I feared they might lead to conflict or discomfort. But Kathleen and I realized that avoiding accountability only allowed problems to fester, creating distance rather than connection. By choosing to face these issues together, we've been able to grow closer and build a stronger foundation for our relationship.

While accountability is essential, it's not always easy. Many couples struggle with being accountable, often because of fear, shame, or ego. It's hard to admit when you've made a mistake or when your actions have hurt your partner. It's even harder when those mistakes are tied to deeper struggles like addictions, past trauma, or unhealthy behaviours.

One of the barriers to accountability is the reluctance to be vulnerable. Admitting weaknesses or mistakes can feel like exposing a part of yourself that you'd rather keep hidden. Kathleen and I have faced this challenge in our own relationship. There were times when I hesitated to share something personal, especially childhood issues that bothered me, because I worried it might change the way she saw me. Similarly, Kathleen sometimes struggled to express her feelings, fearing that I might not understand or validate her emotions.

Another challenge is the temptation to let ego take over. When we're defensive or unwilling to accept responsibility, it's easy to blame our partner or make excuses for our behaviour. But as Kathleen and I have learned, accountability requires humility. It's about setting aside pride and choosing to prioritize the relationship over the need to be "right."

Transparency is a key aspect of accountability, and it's one that Kathleen and I have made a priority in our marriage. We've always believed that trust is the foundation of a healthy relationship, and transparency is the pathway to building that trust.

ACCOUNTABILITY

One practical way we practice transparency is by sharing access to our devices and accounts. This doesn't mean we constantly check each other's phones or invade each other's privacy—it simply means that there are no secrets between us. If Kathleen wants to look at my phone or if I need to use her laptop, there's never a sense of hesitation or suspicion. We've created an environment where transparency is the norm, and this has eliminated the potential for mistrust.

We've also made it a point to discuss personal challenges openly, even when the conversation is uncomfortable. For example, if one of us is struggling with stress, doubts, or temptations, we bring it into the light rather than letting it fester in the dark. These conversations aren't always easy, but they've allowed us to address issues before they escalate and to support each other in moments of vulnerability.

Privacy is important in any relationship, but it should never be used as a shield for secrecy. Kathleen and I have learned that when we approach transparency with love and respect, it becomes a tool for building intimacy and reinforcing our commitment to one another.

Accountability is about more than just avoiding problems—it's about creating a relationship that is resilient, supportive, and built on mutual respect. Without accountability, it's easy for trust to erode and for negative patterns to take root.

For instance, when there is a lack of accountability, individuals may be tempted to engage in behaviours that can harm the relationship, such as visiting inappropriate websites, developing emotional or physical connections with someone outside the marriage, or hiding financial decisions. These behaviours not only damage trust but also create emotional and psychological burdens that can be difficult to overcome.

Kathleen and I have seen firsthand how accountability can resolve issues that might otherwise create division. By addressing challenges openly and working together to find solutions, we've been able to navigate difficult moments without letting them define our relationship.

Whether it's discussing past mistakes, financial decisions, or personal struggles, accountability has been a guiding principle that helps us move forward with clarity and unity.

One of the surprising benefits of accountability is its positive impact on emotional and psychological health. When we avoid accountability, we often carry the weight of unresolved issues—guilt, shame, or regret—that can take a toll on our well-being. But when we choose accountability, we open the door to healing, growth, and freedom.

For Kathleen and me, accountability has been a way to release the burdens of the past and embrace the possibilities of the future. For example, there were times when I struggled with feelings of inadequacy or fear of failure. Instead of hiding these emotions, I shared them with Kathleen, trusting that she would listen without judgment. Her support and encouragement helped me see these struggles not as weaknesses but as opportunities for growth.

Kathleen, too, has experienced the healing power of accountability. By sharing her feelings and experiences openly, she's been able to let go of the pain and doubts that once held her back. Together, we've created a relationship where vulnerability is met with compassion, and this has strengthened not only our connection but also our individual emotional well-being.

Accountability also helps protect relationships from external threats. When couples maintain open communication and a commitment to transparency, they are less likely to fall into patterns of secrecy or temptation. This proactive approach creates a sense of security and stability that benefits both partners.

Practical Steps for Cultivating Accountability

Cultivating accountability in a relationship requires intentional effort and a commitment to growth. Here are some practical steps that Kathleen and I have found helpful:

ACCOUNTABILITY

1. **Create a Safe Space for Communication:** Encourage open and honest conversations where both partners feel heard and valued. Avoid judgment or criticism, and focus on understanding each other's perspectives.
2. **Be Transparent About Challenges:** Share personal struggles, doubts, or temptations with your partner. Transparency builds trust and allows you to address issues together before they escalate.
3. **Set Boundaries and Guidelines:** Establish shared expectations for transparency, such as sharing access to devices or discussing financial decisions. These guidelines create clarity and eliminate potential sources of mistrust.
4. **Acknowledge Mistakes:** When you make a mistake, take responsibility and apologize. Accountability requires humility and a willingness to learn from your actions.
5. **Support Each Other's Growth:** Use accountability as an opportunity to grow together. Encourage your partner, offer support, and celebrate progress, no matter how small.

Accountability is not just a practice—it's a mindset that transforms relationships. For Kathleen and me, it has been the key to building a partnership that is rooted in trust, respect, and mutual support. By embracing transparency, addressing challenges openly, and holding each other accountable, we've created a relationship where growth is possible, even in the face of difficulties.

When couples prioritize accountability, they create a foundation that can withstand the tests of time. They build a relationship that is resilient, emotionally healthy, and deeply connected. As Kathleen and I continue our journey together, we remain committed to the practice of accountability, trusting that it will continue to strengthen our marriage and guide us through every season of life.

DEALING WITH STRUGGLES

Separate The Problem

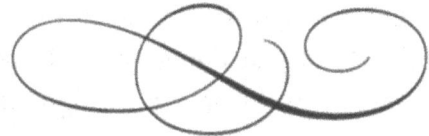

A *king and queen* must learn the art of dealing with struggles while keeping their focus on what truly matters—the strength and unity of their kingdom. If the king begins to see his queen as the problem, he weakens his ability to lead, and if the queen views her king as her obstacle, she loses sight of the wisdom and nurture she brings to their rule. Kathleen and I have had to learn that the problem is never each other—the problem is the challenge we face together. When conflicts arise, we remind ourselves that struggles, though difficult, can be healthy, pushing us to grow, refine our perspectives, and strengthen our relationship.

Instead of allowing difficulties to divide us, we pool our strengths, experiences, and knowledge to find solutions that reinforce our marriage. Separating the problem from the person has been one of the most powerful lessons we've embraced. By standing side by side, rather than against each other, we are able to fight for our marriage, not against

DEALING WITH STRUGGLES

it, ensuring that no obstacle can weaken the kingdom we have built together.

Every marriage faces struggles—moments of uncertainty, disagreements, and challenges that test the bond between two people. Kathleen and I are no exception. Through the years, we've had our fair share of difficulties, both on a personal level and as a couple. But what has sustained us through it all is the unwavering belief that no one can solve our problems but God. He is the center of our union, the foundation of our strength, and the guiding light that shows us the way forward.

From the very early years of our marriage, Kathleen and I made an important decision: we would not discuss our personal struggles with friends or family members. It wasn't because we didn't trust them; it was because we understood that doing so could complicate matters. Friends and family, while well-meaning, might take sides or offer advice shaped by their own biases. Instead, we agreed to seek help from neutral third parties, like therapists, when needed—professionals who could provide objective guidance without being influenced by personal relationships.

This decision proved to be one of the wisest choices we ever made. It allowed us to protect the sanctity of our marriage and gave us the space to work through our struggles in a way that honoured each other. More importantly, it reinforced the belief that the problems were never about *us*—the people God created as His masterpieces. As scripture reminds us, *"For we are God's handiwork, created in Christ Jesus to do good works, which God prepared in advance for us to do"* (Ephesians 2:10, NIV).

Kathleen and I are not the problem; the challenges we face are external, and identifying the root of those challenges is how resolution begins.

Kathleen and I have learned is to separate the problem from the person. It's easy in the heat of the moment to see your spouse as the source of frustration—after all, they're the one standing across from you during a disagreement. But blaming each other only creates division and resentment. Instead, we've made it a habit to focus on the issue at hand, approaching it as a team rather than adversaries.

For example, there was a time when we disagreed about financial priorities. I wanted to invest in a home improvement project, while Kathleen felt we needed to focus on saving for our children's education. At first, the disagreement became heated, with both of us stubbornly holding onto our perspectives. But as we stepped back and prayed for clarity, we realized the problem wasn't *us*—it was the lack of alignment in our financial goals. By identifying the issue, we were able to sit down, share our thoughts honestly, and come up with a solution that honoured both perspectives.

This approach has transformed the way we handle conflicts. Instead of fighting with each other, we put our thoughts together to resolve the problem collaboratively. We've learned that our behaviours, likes and dislikes, perceptions, and opinions may get in the way at times, but getting to the *cause* of the problem is what leads to lasting resolution.

Being honest and open is foundational to dealing with struggles in marriage. Kathleen and I have come to understand that transparency is not just about sharing what's on your mind—it's about creating a safe space where both partners feel heard and valued.

There have been moments in our relationship when honesty was difficult, especially when it involved sharing feedback or criticism. No one enjoys hearing negative critiques, and it's natural to feel defensive. But Kathleen and I realized that avoiding difficult conversations only prolongs the issue and prevents growth. Instead, we've committed to approaching honesty with love and humility, understanding that feedback is not about tearing each other down—it's about building a stronger future together.

For example, Kathleen once shared with me that my extroverted nature sometimes made her feel overwhelmed. As someone who thrives on social interaction, I didn't immediately understand her perspective. But as she explained how constant activity affected her need for quiet reflection, I realized that her honesty was a gift—it was an opportunity for me to grow and adjust my behaviour in a way that honoured her needs.

This experience reinforced the importance of listening. Honesty is only effective when both partners are willing to listen with an open heart, free from judgment or defensiveness. Kathleen and I now approach these conversations as opportunities to strengthen our bond, knowing that mutual understanding is the foundation of a healthy marriage.

When faced with struggles, Kathleen and I have learned to approach problem-solving as a united front. This means setting aside pride, listening to each other's perspectives, and working together to find solutions. It's not always easy—our differences in personality and decision-making styles can create friction—but teamwork is what keeps us moving forward.

One of the strategies we've adopted is taking time to pray before discussing a challenge. Inviting God into the conversation helps us center our thoughts, calms our emotions, and reminds us of the bigger picture. It shifts the focus from "winning" the argument to seeking alignment with God's will.

Another important aspect of problem-solving is acknowledging each other's contributions. Kathleen and I recognize that we both bring unique strengths to the table, and leveraging those strengths is key to finding effective solutions. For instance, Kathleen's introspective nature allows her to think through problems carefully, while my action-oriented personality brings momentum to the decision-making process. By combining these approaches, we're able to tackle challenges with balance and clarity.

Struggles are not roadblocks—they are stepping stones to growth. Kathleen and I have come to view challenges as opportunities to build a stronger future together. Every difficulty we face teaches us something new about ourselves, our relationship, and the God who sustains us.

One of the most profound lessons we've learned is the importance of contribution. As a couple, we are co-laborers in building our future, and both of us must actively participate in problem-solving, decision-making, and growth. This shared responsibility creates a sense of partnership that strengthens our bond and reminds us of our shared purpose.

For Kathleen and me, building a future together means prioritizing what's best for our relationship over individual preferences. It means choosing to forgive, even when forgiveness feels difficult. It means celebrating each other's victories, even when struggles weigh us down. And it means trusting that God is in control, guiding us through every season of life.

Through all of our struggles, Kathleen and I have remained steadfast in one belief: God is the ultimate problem solver. No matter how complex or overwhelming the challenge, He is faithful to provide wisdom, guidance, and peace.

Scripture has been a source of comfort and direction during difficult times. One verse that resonates deeply with us is Proverbs 3:5–6 (NIV): *"Trust in the Lord with all your heart and lean not on your own understanding; in all your ways submit to Him, and He will make your paths straight."*

This reminder to trust God and submit to His will has carried Kathleen and me through moments of doubt, uncertainty, and fear.

DEALING WITH STRUGGLES

We've also learned the power of prayer in resolving struggles. Whether it's asking for clarity, seeking patience, or simply resting in God's presence, prayer connects us to the One who knows our hearts and holds our future. Kathleen and I often pray together, inviting God into our marriage and trusting Him to guide our steps.

While Kathleen and I agreed early in our marriage not to discuss personal struggles with friends or family members, there have been moments when seeking third-party support was necessary. Professional therapists have provided us with valuable insights, helping us navigate challenges with objectivity and wisdom.

Kathleen and I's journey through struggles has been marked by growth, resilience, and unwavering faith. We've learned to identify problems without blaming each other, approach challenges as a team, and rely on God as our ultimate source of strength.

Through honesty, openness, and problem-solving, we've discovered that struggles are not obstacles—they are opportunities to build a future rooted in love, respect, and partnership. Kathleen and I remain committed to moving ahead together, trusting that with God at the center, no challenge is too great to overcome.

OVERCOMING CHALLENGES

Problem-Solve Together

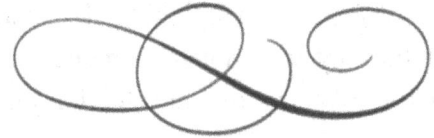

Like dealing with struggles, a *king and queen* had to learn how to overcome challenges, knowing that every obstacle they faced was an opportunity for greater growth. Kathleen and I have discovered that problem-solving together is not just about finding solutions—it's about strengthening our bond, maturing through life's experiences, and deepening our wisdom.

Challenges may feel overwhelming in the moment, but looking back, we see how they shaped us, refined our understanding, and prepared us for the next season. Just as a king and queen use their hardships to build a kingdom of resilience, we have learned to embrace the lessons and wisdom that come with each challenge, knowing that what we endure today is part of the legacy we will pass down to the next generation. That's God's plan for our lives—not to avoid challenges, but to face them together, allowing them to mould us into leaders who build a strong, unshakable foundation for our family.

OVERCOMING CHALLENGES

Every relationship, no matter how deeply rooted in love, faces challenges. Kathleen and I have experienced these moments firsthand, navigating through the ups and downs that come with two people sharing their lives. From unmet expectations to the complexities of communication, relationships are often shaped by the struggles that couples work through together. It is not the absence of challenges that defines a healthy relationship—it is the willingness to confront them, learn from them, and grow stronger as a team.

Kathleen and I quickly learned that expectations can be a double-edged sword. There were times in our marriage when I placed unrealistic expectations on Kathleen—expectations she couldn't meet simply because they didn't align with who she was. Similarly, she had expectations of me that I couldn't fulfill, no matter how hard I tried. This disconnect created frustration and misunderstanding, but over time, we discovered that the key was not to demand perfection from each other but to embrace the beauty of imperfection and work together to find balance.

Some major challenges that many couples face, including those Kathleen and I have encountered in our own journey includes communication, sex and intimacy, trust and many more. Through personal stories, lessons learned, and insights that resonate with lived experiences, we have inspire others to approach their challenges with grace, resilience, and hope.

One of the greatest sources of tension in relationships comes from unmet expectations. When Kathleen and I first married, I assumed she would naturally align with my way of doing things—sharing my enthusiasm for socializing, adopting my communication style, and approaching life with the same level of spontaneity I brought to the table. What I failed to recognize was that Kathleen had her own way of living, shaped by her personality, upbringing, and unique perspective.

For example, I often expected Kathleen to dive into social events with the same energy I did. As an extrovert, I gain energy from being around people, thriving in large gatherings and lively conversations. Kathleen, however, is an introvert who feels drained by prolonged socializing. When we were invited to big events, she would comment, "Your time to shine," signaling that she was there to support me but didn't share my enthusiasm. At first, I took this as a rejection, assuming she wasn't fully invested in our shared experiences. But as we talked openly about her introversion, I realized that her support was an act of love—she was standing by me even when the environment wasn't comfortable for her. Kathleen did not have a name for many years, she was known as "Harrison's wife." Now she is known as a great woman of God, excellent wife and mother.

Kathleen, too, had expectations of me that I struggled to meet. She often hoped I would slow down, reflect more, and take a quieter approach to decision-making. As someone who processes externally and quickly, I found it challenging to adopt her introspective style. But through intentional effort, I learned to appreciate her thoughtfulness and incorporate her perspective into my decisions.

The lesson we've learned is that unmet expectations are not failures—they are opportunities to understand each other better. When couples let go of rigid expectations and focus on valuing their partner's individuality, they create space for growth, compromise, and connection.

Communication is often cited as the cornerstone of a healthy relationship, yet it remains one of the most challenging aspects to master. Kathleen and I have experienced the pitfalls of miscommunication—moments when our words were misunderstood, our intentions misinterpreted, and our emotions left unresolved.

One of the hurdles we've faced is the difference in our communication styles. As someone who speaks openly and directly, I often find it easier to express my thoughts without hesitation. Kathleen, on the other hand, prefers to think through her ideas before speaking, which sometimes leads to delays in sharing her perspective. This mismatch created friction in the early years of our marriage, with me assuming her silence meant disinterest and her perceiving my quick responses as impulsive.

To overcome these challenges, we've worked to find common ground in how we communicate. I've learned to give Kathleen the space she needs to process her thoughts, while she has practiced sharing her perspective more openly. Together, we've developed strategies to ensure that our conversations are productive and respectful, such as asking clarifying questions, paraphrasing each other's words, and checking in to ensure mutual understanding.

One of the most important lessons we've learned is the value of active listening. Communication is not just about speaking—it's about hearing, understanding, and validating your partner's emotions. Kathleen and I now approach conversations with curiosity and empathy, creating a safe space for honest dialogue.

Trust and respect are the foundation of any successful relationship, but they are not immune to the challenges couples face. Kathleen and I have had moments when past hurts and mistakes resurfaced, bringing tension and doubt into our bond. These moments required intentional effort to rebuild trust and strengthen respect.

One struggle we've encountered is the tendency to bring up old wounds during disagreements. It's a common dynamic in relationships—when emotions run high, past mistakes can resurface as a way to "win" an argument or deflect accountability. Kathleen and I quickly realized that this pattern was damaging, eroding trust and making reconciliation more difficult.

To address this challenge, we've committed to resolving issues without revisiting past hurts. Instead, we focus on the present, asking questions like, "What is the core issue here?" and "How can we move forward together?" This approach allows us to build trust through transparency and mutual accountability, rather than reliving old pain.

Respect also plays a crucial role in overcoming challenges. Kathleen and I have learned that respect is not just about being polite—it's about valuing each other's perspectives, honouring boundaries, and recognizing the contributions each partner brings to the relationship. When respect is present, trust becomes easier to nurture, creating a partnership that thrives on mutual understanding.

Relationships are often impacted by external pressures, such as work-related stress, parenting challenges, financial difficulties, and mental health struggles. Kathleen and I have faced all of these at various points in our marriage, learning to navigate them together rather than allowing them to create division.

One particularly challenging season came when both of us were juggling demanding careers while raising our children. The constant pressure to excel at work, manage household responsibilities, and be present for our family left us feeling exhausted and disconnected. Kathleen often felt overwhelmed, while I struggled to balance my drive for success with the need to be emotionally available.

To navigate this season, we prioritized teamwork and support. Kathleen and I divided responsibilities based on our strengths, sought help from trusted mentors, and practiced self-care to ensure that our stress didn't overshadow our bond. We also made time for each other, carving out moments of connection amidst the busyness of life.

Stress is inevitable, but how couples respond to it makes all the difference. Kathleen and I have found that approaching external pressures as a team—rather than as individuals—strengthens our resilience and reinforces our commitment to each other.

OVERCOMING CHALLENGES

Many couples face challenges in their sexual intimacy and romantic life, and Kathleen and I are no exception. Over the years, the demands of parenting, work, and everyday life sometimes left us feeling distant, with little time or energy to nurture physical and emotional intimacy.

To address this challenge, we've made an intentional effort to reignite our connection. Kathleen and I have learned the importance of prioritizing romance, whether it's through date nights, small gestures of affection, or simply spending quality time together. Creating space for intimacy has allowed us to deepen our bond and strengthen the emotional foundation of our relationship. I plan to write a book on "I paid $147.00 for sex." With the children being awake and living in a small house, sex was difficult to enjoy. Once a month, I paid $147.00 at a hotel to enjoy the company of Kathleen, with dinner and enjoyable intimacy.

One lesson we've learned is that intimacy is not just about physical connection—it's about emotional vulnerability, trust, and mutual care. Kathleen and I have found that discussing our needs openly and honouring each other's boundaries creates a safe and loving environment where intimacy can thrive.

Raising children is one of the most rewarding yet challenging aspects of a relationship. Kathleen and I have experienced the ups and downs of parenting, from sleepless nights to moments of profound joy. Navigating these challenges as a team has been essential to maintaining a healthy relationship.

One of the difficulties we've faced is differing parenting styles. Kathleen's thoughtful approach often focuses on nurturing our children's emotional needs, while my action-oriented style emphasizes discipline and structure. At times, these differences have led to disagreements about how to address certain situations.

To overcome these challenges, we've worked to find balance in our parenting methods. Kathleen and I now approach parenting decisions collaboratively, ensuring that both perspectives are considered. We've also made an effort to support each other, recognizing that parenting is a shared responsibility that requires teamwork and grace.

Challenges in relationships are inevitable, but Kathleen and I have learned that they can be opportunities for growth, connection, and resilience. By addressing unmet expectations, fostering open communication, rebuilding trust, and navigating external pressures as a team, we've discovered the strength of our partnership and the beauty of working through difficulties together.

Every couple faces unique struggles, but the principles of patience, empathy, and collaboration remain universal. Kathleen and I continue to approach our challenges with a spirit of hope, trusting that God's guidance will sustain us through every season of life. As we navigate the complexities of relationships, we remain committed to building a future rooted in love, respect, and unwavering support.

OVERCOMING CHALLENGES

NOT SEEING THINGS EYE TO EYE

The Power of Agreeing to Disagree

A *king and queen* may not always see things eye to eye, but they must learn the strength that comes with agreeing to disagree. Leadership within a kingdom—or a marriage—is never about winning arguments; it's about honouring each other's perspectives while keeping unity intact. Kathleen and I have had to embrace this truth in our own relationship, recognizing that differences do not make us opponents—they make us stronger when handled with wisdom.

There have been times when I've had strong opinions or when Kathleen's perspective challenged mine, but we learned that as long as our disagreements do not compromise our faith, godly principles, morals, or integrity, they can be opportunities for growth rather than division. Instead of making impulsive decisions in moments of disagreement, we let things sit, seek counsel when needed, and ground our discussions in truth and wisdom rather than emotion.

History shows that kings and queens who ruled wisely never allowed personal differences to weaken their leadership. They understood that love and respect must remain greater than any disagreement. Kathleen and I have followed that same principle, knowing that even if we don't always see things the same way, our love and commitment must always be stronger than our differences.

Marriage, as rich and beautiful as it is, is also an intricate dance of two individuals bringing their unique thoughts, perspectives, and preferences into a shared space. Naturally, it is impossible to see eye to eye on every single issue. Kathleen and I have certainly had our fair share of disputes and disagreements over the years. The key to navigating these moments is not about trying to erase differences or always reaching total agreement. Instead, it's about acknowledging those differences with respect and, when necessary, agreeing to disagree.

As a "king" and "queen" of our home, it is crucial for both partners to lead with grace and humility when conflicts arise. Kathleen and I have learned that disputes are not signs of a broken relationship but opportunities to deepen our understanding of each other. Agreeing to disagree doesn't mean giving up—it means building bridges of respect and trust that allow both partners to move forward in unity, even when their opinions diverge.

One of the first lessons Kathleen and I learned in marriage was that disagreements are completely natural. We come from different backgrounds, have distinct personalities, and approach life in our own unique ways. When you think about it, expecting two individuals to agree on everything is unrealistic. Our individuality is what makes us who we are—and what makes our relationship vibrant and full of depth.

Early in our marriage, I often felt frustrated when Kathleen didn't immediately agree with me on decisions, both big and small. As someone who thrives on decisiveness and action, I wanted quick resolutions, while Kathleen preferred to take her time, think deeply, and consider all angles. There were moments when these differences led to tension, especially when I felt that her slower pace was holding us back, and she felt that my urgency was overwhelming.

But over time, we realized that these moments of disagreement were not about one of us being right and the other being wrong—they were about two perspectives that needed to coexist. Instead of seeing disagreement as a roadblock, we began to see it as an opportunity to learn from each other. Kathleen's deliberation taught me patience and consideration, while my decisiveness encouraged her to embrace action and confidence.

One of the most transformative lessons we've learned is to focus on the problem, not the person. Disagreements can easily spiral into arguments when the focus shifts from the issue at hand to personal criticisms. For example, during one of our debates about finances early in our marriage, I blurted out something along the lines of, "You're always overly cautious!" Kathleen, in turn, felt attacked and responded defensively. The issue—whether to spend or save—was soon overshadowed by hurt feelings.

We eventually realized that if we were going to navigate disagreements effectively, we needed to stop pointing fingers and start addressing the actual problem. Instead of saying, "You're being too cautious," I learned to say, "I see your point about saving, but I think we should also consider this opportunity." These subtle shifts in language helped us approach disagreements as teammates rather than opponents.

Disagreements are not battles to be won; they are puzzles to be solved. When couples focus on understanding the issue instead of assigning blame, they create a space for collaborative problem-solving. Kathleen and I have found that when we approach conflicts with curiosity and humility, we're able to reach resolutions that honour both of our perspectives.

Respect is the cornerstone of agreeing to disagree. Without it, disagreements can quickly turn toxic, leaving both partners feeling unheard and undervalued. Kathleen and I have worked hard to cultivate a culture of respect in our marriage, especially during moments of conflict.

One way we practice respect is by giving each other the space to express our thoughts and feelings without interruption. For example, if Kathleen feels strongly about an issue, I make it a point to listen fully before responding, even if I disagree. Similarly, she gives me the same courtesy when I need to share my perspective. This simple act of listening helps us feel valued and respected, even when our opinions don't align.

We've also learned to validate each other's feelings, even when we don't see things the same way. For instance, there was a time when I wanted to make a significant career change that Kathleen wasn't entirely comfortable with. While she didn't initially agree with my decision, she took the time to understand my motivations and assured me that my feelings were valid. In turn, I acknowledged her concerns and worked to address them. This mutual respect allowed us to navigate the disagreement with grace and unity.

Respect doesn't mean always agreeing; it means honouring your partner's voice and valuing their perspective as an essential part of the relationship.

There are moments in every marriage when no amount of discussion or compromise can bridge the gap between two perspectives. In these instances, agreeing to disagree becomes a vital tool for maintaining harmony and moving forward.

For Kathleen and me, agreeing to disagree is not about avoidance or resignation—it's about acknowledging that our relationship is bigger than any single issue. It's a way of saying, "We may not see eye to eye on this, but we still respect and love each other."

For example, we've had different views on parenting decisions over the years. There was a time when I felt strongly about introducing certain activities into our children's lives, while Kathleen felt that they needed more unstructured time to explore their interests. After many discussions, we realized that neither of us was entirely right or wrong—our perspectives were simply different. We agreed to disagree, allowing each of us to bring our unique strengths to the parenting journey.

The key to agreeing to disagree is ensuring that it doesn't create lingering resentment. Kathleen and I make it a point to revisit these topics periodically, checking in to see if our perspectives have shifted or if new solutions have emerged. This approach helps us stay connected and prevents unresolved disagreements from festering.

As the "king" and "queen" of our home, Kathleen and I recognize that leadership in marriage is a shared responsibility. Disagreements can often arise when one partner feels their role or perspective is being undermined. To address this, we've adopted a mindset of mutual leadership, where both voices carry equal weight.

For example, when it comes to financial decisions, Kathleen often brings a cautious, detail-oriented perspective, while I provide a broader, goal-driven approach. Instead of trying to dominate the conversation, we work together to ensure that both perspectives are represented in our decisions. This balance of leadership allows us to navigate disagreements with respect and collaboration, rather than competition.

The king and queen dynamic reminds us that marriage is not about power struggles—it's about partnership. When both partners feel empowered to lead and contribute, disagreements become opportunities for growth rather than sources of division.

NOT SEEING THINGS EYE TO EYE

Disagreements, while challenging, are also opportunities for growth. Kathleen and I have found that working through conflicts has strengthened our relationship, teaching us valuable lessons about ourselves and each other.

For example, I've learned to appreciate Kathleen's introspective nature, even when it contrasts with my quick decision-making style. She has taught me the value of patience and reflection, helping me approach decisions with greater thoughtfulness. Similarly, Kathleen has learned to embrace my spontaneity, finding joy in the unexpected and stepping outside her comfort zone.

Every disagreement we've navigated has brought us closer, reminding us that our differences are not obstacles—they are gifts. By embracing these moments as opportunities for growth, we've deepened our understanding of each other and strengthened our bond.

Not seeing things eye to eye is a natural part of any relationship, but it doesn't have to create division. For Kathleen and me, disagreements have become opportunities to practice respect, humility, and teamwork. By agreeing to disagree, we've learned to honour each other's perspectives and navigate conflicts with grace.

As the king and queen of our home, we recognize that our relationship is built on a foundation of shared love and mutual respect. Even when our opinions diverge, our commitment to each other remains unwavering. Through open communication, active listening, and a willingness to compromise, we've discovered the beauty of unity through diversity.

Agreeing to disagree is not a sign of weakness—it's a testament to the strength of a relationship. It's a reminder that love is not about erasing differences but embracing them, building a partnership that thrives on understanding and collaboration. As Kathleen and I continue this journey together, we remain committed to honouring each other's voices and working as a team to build a future full of love, respect, and harmony.

NOT SEEING THINGS EYE TO EYE

EMOTIONS AND RATIONALIZATIONS

Balancing Emotional and Rational Personalities

Emotions and rationalizations have always played a vital role in leadership and relationships, shaping decisions and guiding interactions. A *king* may have been taught to suppress his emotions, relying solely on logic, facts, and reason to rule his kingdom, while a *queen* may have been more in tune with emotional insight, leading with heart and intuition. But neither approach is complete on its own—emotions are valuable when channeled wisely, and rationalization is necessary to build a foundation of stability.

A kingdom cannot be built purely on emotions, nor can it thrive solely on rigid logic—it requires both to function effectively. Kathleen and I have learned this lesson in our marriage, understanding that balancing emotions with rational thought protects our relationship and strengthens our family. We allow emotions to shape how we relate to one another, ensuring that love, understanding, and empathy remain at the heart of every decision. At the same time, we rely on rationalization to make firm choices, ensuring that our actions align with wisdom and long-term stability. A marriage, just like a kingdom, flourishes when passion is guided by reason, and reason is softened by love.

Marriage is a beautiful union of two unique individuals, each bringing their own personality, traits, and worldview into the relationship. In many cases, these differences can complement one another, creating a dynamic partnership built on balance. However, when one partner is more emotional and the other is more rational, challenges can arise that test the foundation of the relationship. For Kathleen and me, this dynamic was very much a part of our early years. Kathleen's emotional nature was often guided by her heart, while I leaned more on logic and rationality in decision-making. These differences occasionally created tension, but they also shaped the story of how we learned to rule our "kingdom" together.

What we've come to understand over time is that the interplay between emotion and rationality doesn't have to create division—it can lead to balance, harmony, and growth when managed with grace and understanding. In this chapter, I'll share how Kathleen and I navigated this dynamic, what we learned along the way, and how balancing emotion and rationality has strengthened our marriage and our family.

When we talk about marriage as a "kingdom," it's not just metaphorical. Kathleen and I believe that a strong marriage establishes a legacy not just for the couple but for their children and future generations. A kingdom needs both leadership and compassion, rules and grace, logic and emotion. A king and queen must work together, balancing their strengths and compensating for each other's weaknesses, to create a harmonious environment where love, respect, and unity thrive.

In our marriage, Kathleen's emotional intelligence brought warmth and connection to our kingdom. She was always attuned to the needs of our children, our extended family, and even our neighbors. Her empathy allowed her to nurture relationships in ways I hadn't even thought of. On the other hand, my rational approach provided structure and stability. I was the planner, the one who focused on financial security, long-term goals, and decision-making processes that set the foundation for our future.

This dynamic might sound ideal, but in practice, it wasn't always easy. When differences arose, we struggled to find common ground. Kathleen's tears in the early days of our marriage made it difficult for her to express her needs without being overwhelmed by emotion, and my hyper-focus on logic sometimes made me dismissive of her feelings. There were times when I would get frustrated, thinking, "Why can't she just look at the facts?" while she wondered, "Why doesn't he understand how I feel?"

Our differences became especially apparent when it came to finances. I remember vividly how I once hid $10,000 from Kathleen early in our marriage. My rationale was simple: I feared that her emotional nature would lead her to spend the money impulsively or give it away to someone in need. I didn't see this as deceitful at the time; rather, I thought of it as protecting our financial future. Kathleen, on the other hand, saw money as a tool for caring for others—a way to express love, generosity, and connection.

Looking back, I realize that my decision to hide the money was not a reflection of Kathleen's character but of my own lack of trust and understanding. I had allowed my fear of "what could happen" to dictate my actions, failing to consider how my secrecy would affect our relationship. When Kathleen eventually found out, it led to a deep conversation about trust, communication, and the need to respect each other's perspectives.

EMOTIONS AND RATIONALIZATIONS

This experience taught me that while my rationality could be a strength, it could also be a limitation if it wasn't balanced by empathy. Kathleen helped me see that her emotional connection to money wasn't reckless—it was rooted in her deep desire to care for others and make a difference. In turn, I helped her understand that financial planning and discipline were necessary to ensure that we could provide for our family's future. Together, we found a middle ground that honoured both of our perspectives.

Over time, and with the wisdom that comes from maturity and experience, Kathleen and I learned to embrace our differences as strengths rather than weaknesses. Instead of viewing her emotional nature as a liability, I began to see it as a source of compassion and insight. Similarly, Kathleen stopped viewing my rational approach as cold or unfeeling, recognizing that it provided stability and direction for our family.

One of the turning points for me was seeing how our children viewed us. While I had always thought of myself as the rational one in the marriage, my kids would often point out how emotional I had become, especially during significant moments like their weddings. Watching my children get married brought tears to my eyes every time, reminding me that emotions are not weaknesses—they are a reflection of love, pride, and connection.

Kathleen, too, grew in her ability to balance emotion with rationality. She learned to step back and consider the facts when making decisions, ensuring that her compassion was paired with practicality. Together, we created a partnership where both logic and emotion had a place, allowing us to navigate challenges with wisdom and grace.

What we've learned through our journey is that God designed us with both emotions and rationality for a reason. Emotions are a gift—they allow us to connect, empathize, and experience the depth of human relationships. Rationality, on the other hand, is a tool for making sound decisions, solving problems, and building a stable future. When these two aspects are balanced, they create a foundation for a healthy and thriving relationship.

Scripture speaks to the importance of this balance. Ecclesiastes 3:1 (NIV) reminds us that *"There is a time for everything, and a season for every activity under the heavens."*

This includes a time for emotion and a time for logic, a time to feel and a time to think. Recognizing when to lean into one or the other is part of the wisdom that comes with growing together in marriage.

For Kathleen and me, learning to balance emotions and rationality has been a process of listening to God's guidance and trusting that His design for our partnership is intentional. We've come to see that our differences are not obstacles but opportunities to reflect His love and creativity in our marriage.

One of the most important areas where balance is crucial is in making tough decisions. As the king and queen of our home, Kathleen and I are often faced with choices that affect not just us but our entire family. These moments require us to bring both emotion and rationality to the table, ensuring that our decisions are guided by both compassion and wisdom.

For example, when one of our children faced a challenging situation at school, Kathleen's emotional response was to protect and comfort, while my rational side wanted to address the issue head-on with practical solutions. At first, our approaches seemed at odds, but as we talked and prayed together, we realized that both perspectives were needed. Kathleen's empathy helped our child feel supported and understood, while my logical approach provided actionable steps to resolve the issue. Together, we were able to navigate the situation in a way that honoured both our child's feelings and their needs.

EMOTIONS AND RATIONALIZATIONS

These experiences have taught us the importance of balancing each other out. When Kathleen leads with her heart, I provide the structure and stability to back her up. When I approach a situation with logic, she brings the warmth and connection that ensure our decisions are rooted in love. By standing together and respecting each other's strengths, we create a partnership that is greater than the sum of its parts.

Lessons for Healthy Relationships

Our journey has been filled with lessons that have shaped the way we approach our marriage. Here are some of the key takeaways that have helped Kathleen and me build a balanced and healthy relationship:

1. **Embrace Differences:** Instead of trying to change each other, celebrate the unique strengths that each partner brings to the relationship. Emotions and rationality are both gifts that can complement one another when embraced with respect.
2. **Communicate Openly:** Balancing emotion and rationality requires open and honest communication. Share your thoughts, feelings, and perspectives without fear of judgment, and listen to your partner with empathy and understanding.
3. **Trust God's Design:** Remember that God created both partners with unique qualities for a reason. Trust that your differences are part of His plan for your marriage and seek His guidance in navigating challenges.
4. **Work Together on Tough Decisions:** When faced with difficult choices, bring both emotion and logic to the table. Collaborate as a team to ensure that your decisions reflect both compassion and wisdom.
5. **Celebrate Growth:** Recognize and celebrate the ways you've grown together as a couple. Whether it's learning to balance your differences or navigating challenges with grace, every step forward is a testament to the strength of your partnership.

Kathleen and I's journey of balancing emotion and rationality has been one of growth, understanding, and love. While our differences once felt like challenges, they have become the strengths that define our partnership. Together, we've learned to stand as king and queen, ruling our kingdom with both heart and wisdom.

Our children have seen this balance in action, and it's our hope that they carry these lessons into their own relationships. By embracing both emotion and logic, they too can build partnerships that reflect God's design for unity and love.

As Kathleen and I continue this journey together, we remain committed to honouring each other's strengths, trusting God's plan, and building a legacy of balance and harmony in our marriage.

EMOTIONS AND RATIONALIZATIONS

STRENGTHS AND WEAKNESSES

Nothing Is Wasted

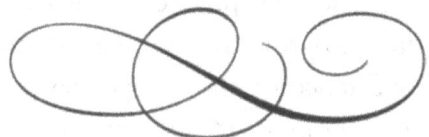

A *king and queen* understand that strengths and weaknesses exist in every individual, but the key to effective leadership—whether in ruling a kingdom or nurturing a marriage—is knowing how to maximize strengths and use weaknesses as opportunities for growth. No one is perfect, and the most successful rulers are those who recognize that they don't know everything, yet remain humble enough to learn.

Kathleen and I have come to understand that nothing is wasted—every strength is meant to be celebrated, and every weakness offers a chance to improve. Just as a king and queen rely on their advisors and trusted supporters to fill in the gaps, we lean on each other and those around us to ensure that our responsibilities are met. Wisdom is not in denying weakness, but in knowing how to handle it with grace. We have

STRENGTHS AND WEAKNESSES

learned that our strengths make us shine, and our weaknesses make us grow—and when handled well, this is a win-win situation for us, our family, and the life we are building together.

Marriage is a journey of two individuals, each bringing their unique strengths and weaknesses to the partnership. While these differences can enrich a relationship, they can also be the source of tension if not approached with understanding and grace. Kathleen and I, like many couples, have faced moments where we struggled to see past each other's weaknesses. It's natural to focus on the one wrong thing your spouse may do, especially when emotions are heightened, rather than appreciating the countless positive qualities they bring to the relationship. However, through reflection, maturity, and intentional effort, we learned that focusing on strengths—not weaknesses—creates the foundation for a thriving marriage.

Kathleen and I embrace the practice of appreciating each other's strengths while learning to grow through our weaknesses. Our journey has taught us the importance of shifting perspective, choosing battles wisely, and building a culture of respect and appreciation. The impact of focusing on strengths, navigating through weaknesses with empathy, and the practical steps couples can foster a healthy, balanced partnership.

One of the greatest challenges couple's faces is the tendency to magnify their spouse's weaknesses while minimizing their strengths. Early in our marriage, I found myself falling into this trap more often than I'd like to admit. Kathleen would do ninety-nine wonderful things for our family—managing the household, nurturing our children, supporting my career—and yet I would fixate on the one mistake or shortcoming that affected me. Perhaps she forgot something important or made a decision I didn't agree with, and my mind would focus solely on that.

It's a slippery slope. When we constantly dwell on weaknesses, they consume our thoughts, shaping how we view our spouse and the relationship. This negative mindset can lead to frustration, resentment, and even separation. It's like the analogy of the pink donuts—when you tell yourself not to think about them, they become all you can focus on. Similarly, the more we focus on our spouse's shortcomings, the harder it becomes to see their positive qualities.

Kathleen and I had to break this cycle before it took a toll on our marriage. We realized that our weaknesses didn't define us—they were simply part of who we are. By choosing to focus on each other's strengths, we shifted our perspective from criticism to appreciation, creating a culture of gratitude and positivity in our relationship.

One of the most transformative practices Kathleen and I adopted was the intentional effort to identify each other's strengths. This exercise helped us reframe our mindset, reminding us of the positive contributions we each bring to the relationship.

For Kathleen, her strengths are numerous—she is compassionate, nurturing, and emotionally intelligent. She has an incredible ability to connect with people, whether it's comforting our children during difficult moments or offering support to friends and family. Her servant-hearted nature shines in everything she does, from cooking meals for others to planning thoughtful surprises that bring joy to those around her.

As for me, my strengths lie in leadership, problem-solving, and providing stability for our family. I'm goal-oriented and practical, ensuring that we stay on track with our plans and priorities. While Kathleen brings warmth and connection, I provide structure and direction, creating a partnership that is both dynamic and grounded.

When Kathleen and I took the time to identify these strengths, it shifted the way we approached our relationship. Instead of focusing on weaknesses, we began to celebrate what made each of us unique.

STRENGTHS AND WEAKNESSES

Serving, emotional support, companionship, and care are gifts that cannot be measured by monetary value. They are the pillars of a healthy marriage, and recognizing them strengthens the bond between partners.

Another important lesson Kathleen and I learned was to choose our battles wisely. In marriage, disagreements are inevitable, but not every issue needs to be a source of conflict. By identifying what truly matters and letting go of minor irritations, couples can avoid unnecessary tension and focus on building their relationship.

For example, there were moments when Kathleen's emotional nature led to decisions I didn't fully agree with. Early in our marriage, I would confront these situations head-on, often escalating the conflict. But as I matured, I realized that many of these "battles" weren't worth fighting. Kathleen's intentions were always rooted in love and care, and her decisions, even if different from my own, rarely caused any harm.

Kathleen, too, learned to assess which disagreements were worth pursuing. While my rational approach sometimes frustrated her, she recognized that my goal was always to protect our family's well-being. Instead of pointing fingers or dwelling on mistakes, Kathleen began to approach disagreements with curiosity, asking questions to understand my perspective.

Choosing battles wisely doesn't mean avoiding conflict—it means addressing issues with intention and respect. Kathleen and I now approach disagreements with a collaborative mindset, focusing on resolution rather than blame.

Weaknesses are part of every relationship, but they don't have to be sources of division. Kathleen and I have learned that navigating weaknesses requires empathy, understanding, and a commitment to growth.

One of my weaknesses, as Kathleen often reminds me, is my tendency to focus on details, especially when it comes to finances. I'm the type of person who notices if five cents are missing from a receipt and will go back to the store to resolve it. While this trait reflects my commitment to accountability, it sometimes creates tension when Kathleen wants to prioritize generosity or flexibility.

Kathleen's weakness, on the other hand, is her emotional sensitivity, which can sometimes make her feel overwhelmed during disagreements. Early in our marriage, her tears during arguments made it difficult for us to communicate effectively, as I struggled to balance my rational approach with her emotional needs.

To navigate these weaknesses, Kathleen and I adopted a mindset of growth. We stopped pointing fingers and began working together to address the root causes of our struggles. I learned to balance my attention to detail with flexibility, recognizing when it's better to let go and trust Kathleen's instincts. Kathleen, in turn, grew in her ability to manage her emotions during disagreements, allowing us to have productive conversations even in challenging moments.

Growth takes time, but with patience and empathy, couples can turn weaknesses into opportunities for connection and resilience.

Appreciation is one of the most powerful tools for building a strong and lasting marriage. When Kathleen and I began focusing on each other's strengths and expressing gratitude for the positives, it transformed the way we interacted with one another.

For example, I make it a point to thank Kathleen for her support, whether it's her thoughtful advice during a difficult decision or her ability to create a warm and inviting home. Kathleen, in turn, expresses appreciation for my leadership, reminding me that my efforts to provide stability for our family are deeply valued.

These expressions of gratitude may seem small, but they have a profound impact. They remind us of the love and respect we share, even when challenges arise. Appreciation creates a culture of positivity,

STRENGTHS AND WEAKNESSES

reinforcing the belief that our marriage is built on mutual support and understanding.

According to Emmons and McCullough (2021), practicing gratitude in relationships enhances emotional well-being and strengthens interpersonal connections. Kathleen and I have found that this principle holds true—our intentional effort to appreciate each other's strengths has deepened our bond and fostered a sense of unity in our marriage.

Practical Steps for Appreciating Strengths

Couples who want to cultivate appreciation in their relationship can start with simple yet meaningful practices. Here are some steps Kathleen and I have adopted that may be helpful to others:

1. **Make a Strengths List:** Take time to write down your spouse's strengths, highlighting the qualities that enrich your relationship. Reflect on this list during moments of frustration to shift your focus from weaknesses to positives.
2. **Express Gratitude Daily:** Make it a habit to thank your spouse for their contributions, whether big or small. Regular expressions of appreciation reinforce the bond between partners.
3. **Practice Empathy:** Seek to understand your spouse's perspective, especially when their actions or decisions differ from your own. Empathy fosters connection and reduces tension.
4. **Choose Battles Wisely:** Assess which disagreements are worth pursuing and let go of minor irritations. Focus on building unity rather than creating division.
5. **Invest in Growth:** Work together to address weaknesses, supporting each other's efforts to grow and improve. Celebrate progress, no matter how small.

Kathleen and I's journey of appreciating each other's weaknesses and strengths has been one of growth, transformation, and love. By shifting our focus from criticism to gratitude, we've built a marriage that thrives on respect, empathy, and understanding. When couples celebrate each other's positives and navigate weaknesses with grace, they create a partnership that is resilient and enriching. Kathleen and I remain committed to practicing gratitude, trusting that it will continue to strengthen our bond and sustain our "kingdom" for years to come.

STRENGTHS AND WEAKNESSES

APPRECIATE PRESSURE

The Catalyst for Growth

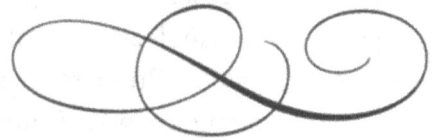

A *king and queen* must learn to appreciate pressure, understanding that it is not meant to break them, but to shape them into stronger leaders. Pressure is an unavoidable part of ruling—expectations from the people they govern, demands from each other, and the weight of decisions that impact their kingdom. But instead of seeing pressure as a burden, wise rulers recognize that it is a catalyst for growth, pushing them to think rationally, act wisely, and make decisions based on logic rather than emotion.

Kathleen and I have embraced this same principle in our marriage. When life places heavy demands on us—whether in our relationship, parenting, or personal challenges—we remind ourselves that pressure does not last forever. It may feel overwhelming in the moment, but with the right mindset, it becomes a tool for transformation, forcing us to refine our approach, strengthen our resilience, and grow into better

APPRECIATE PRESSURE

versions of ourselves. Growth is never comfortable, but it is always worth it.

Pressure is often perceived as a burden, something to avoid or escape. Yet, Kathleen and I have come to understand that pressure, when embraced, has the power to propel us forward. It takes strong pressure to move things, much like the force of water traveling through a hose. Pressure, far from being a negative force, has been the driving force behind our personal, spiritual, and relational growth. Everything we've achieved together—the jobs we've landed, the finances we've balanced, and the challenges we've overcome—was made possible because of pressure.

Our journey has shown us that the weight of pressure, though difficult at times, refines us, strengthens us, and pushes us beyond our comfort zones. It compels us to make decisions, take action, and grow in ways we never thought possible. Pressure shapes our lives and teaches us the lessons we learn along the way. Embracing pressure has led to some of our most significant breakthroughs.

Kathleen and I are where we are today because of pressure. In the early years of our marriage, pressure was a constant companion, urging us to move forward and take steps that might otherwise have seemed daunting. Whether it was finding jobs, disciplining our children, or balancing our finances, pressure forced us to evaluate our priorities, make tough decisions, and take action.

One of the most challenging yet pivotal moments in our lives came when I decided to go back to school in my 30s. At that time, we were raising seven children, pastoring a church, running a Bible college, and I was driving a school bus to make ends meet. Despite our best efforts, our income wasn't enough to sustain our growing family. With nine mouths to feed and bills piling up, the pressure to create a better future was immense. Going back to school was a tough decision—one that required sacrifices, hard work, and faith. But it was also one of the best decisions we ever made.

Pressure has a way of pushing us past procrastination. It eliminates the luxury of "someday" and forces us to confront the reality of now. Kathleen and I learned that when we embrace pressure as a motivator rather than a hindrance, it becomes a tool for progress. It propels us to set goals, take risks, and pursue opportunities that lead to growth.

Pressure also has a way of refining our priorities. During the seasons when money was tight and resources were limited, Kathleen and I learned the importance of distinguishing between wants and needs. This wasn't always easy, especially with seven children who had their own desires and dreams. But pressure forced us to discipline ourselves and make decisions that prioritized what truly mattered.

For example, we had to learn to say "no" to unnecessary expenses and focus on the essentials—paying the mortgage, putting food on the table, and ensuring our children had what they needed to thrive. This wasn't just about financial discipline; it was about teaching our children the value of gratitude, contentment, and resourcefulness. We wanted them to understand that true happiness doesn't come from material possessions but from the love, faith, and unity that binds a family together.

Pressure also taught us the power of delayed gratification. There were times when we had to put our own desires on hold to ensure our family's stability. Yet, these sacrifices didn't feel like burdens—they felt like investments in the future we were building together. Looking back, we see how these moments of pressure shaped our character and strengthened our resolve.

Just as pressure is needed to clean dirt, stains, and even garbage, it also has the power to cleanse our lives. Kathleen and I have faced moments when pressure forced us to confront past mistakes, wrong choices, and regrets. These moments were not easy, but they were necessary for our growth.

There were times in our marriage when unresolved issues from the past threatened to hold us back. Whether it was financial mistakes, unmet expectations, or lingering hurts, pressure created the urgency to address these challenges head-on. Instead of burying our struggles or avoiding difficult conversations, we leaned into the discomfort, trusting that God would guide us through the process of healing and restoration.

Pressure also helped us let go of the pain that was no longer serving us. Holding onto resentment or regret only weighed us down, preventing us from moving forward. But when we allowed pressure to refine us, it became a catalyst for forgiveness, renewal, and growth. We learned that letting go is not a sign of weakness—it's a step toward freedom.

Perhaps the most profound lesson we've learned is how pressure strengthens faith. There was a season in our lives when we were paying a $1,700 mortgage each month, plus utilities, vehicle insurance, food, and clothing, all on an annual income of $22,000. On paper, it didn't make sense how we could make ends meet. Yet, we saw God work miracles in our lives, stretching our resources in ways we couldn't explain.

One of the reasons we were able to persevere was our commitment to faithful giving. Despite the financial pressures we faced, Kathleen and I made it a priority to give to others and honour God with our resources. This wasn't always easy—it required trust and a willingness to surrender our fears. But time and time again, we saw how God provided for our needs, often in unexpected ways.

Pressure has a way of revealing where our faith truly lies. It strips away self-reliance and reminds us of our dependence on God's grace and provision. Kathleen and I have learned that when we embrace pressure with faith, it becomes an opportunity to witness God's power and experience His faithfulness.

Pressure doesn't just move us forward—it transforms us. It pushes us to grow in ways we never thought possible, challenging us to rise above our circumstances and become stronger, wiser, and more resilient.

For Kathleen and me, growth through pressure has taken many forms. It has strengthened our marriage, deepened our faith, and taught us the value of perseverance. It has shown us that even in the midst of challenges, there is beauty to be found and lessons to be learned.

One area where pressure has refined us is in parenting. Raising seven children comes with its own set of pressures—from managing schedules to navigating conflicts and guiding them through life's challenges. Yet, these pressures have also brought immense joy and fulfillment. They've taught us patience, empathy, and the importance of leading by example.

Pressure has also shaped our perspectives on success and contentment. It has reminded us that true success is not measured by wealth or status but by the relationships we nurture, the values we uphold, and the legacy we leave behind.

One of the greatest gifts of pressure is its ability to reveal purpose. When Kathleen and I look back on our journey, we see how moments of pressure—though difficult at the time—led us to places of growth, transformation, and blessing. Whether it was pursuing education in my 30s, navigating financial challenges, or confronting past mistakes, each experience of pressure brought us closer to the life we were meant to live.

We've also come to see pressure as an opportunity to serve others. Our experiences have given us a deeper understanding of what it means to persevere, trust, and grow, and we've been able to share these lessons with others who are facing similar challenges. Pressure has not only shaped our lives—it has equipped us to be a source of encouragement and hope for others.

APPRECIATE PRESSURE

Practical Lessons for Embracing Pressure

Here are some practical lessons Kathleen and I have learned about embracing pressure:

1. **Change Your Perspective:** Instead of viewing pressure as a burden, see it as an opportunity for growth. Pressure can refine your character and push you toward your goals.
2. **Prioritize What Matters:** Pressure can help you clarify your priorities. Focus on what truly matters, and let go of what doesn't.
3. **Rely on Faith:** Trust that God will provide the strength and resources you need to navigate pressure. Faith turns challenges into opportunities for miracles.
4. **Work as a Team:** Facing pressure together strengthens your bond as a couple. Support each other, communicate openly, and approach challenges as a united front.
5. **Celebrate Growth:** Recognize the ways pressure has shaped you and brought you closer to your goals. Celebrate the victories, no matter how small.

Pressure is not something to be feared—it is something to be appreciated. Kathleen and I are living proof of how pressure can lead to growth, transformation, and blessing. It has propelled us forward, refined our priorities, strengthened our faith, and revealed our purpose.

When couples embrace pressure with trust and determination, they discover the beauty of what lies on the other side. Kathleen and I remain grateful for the pressures we've faced, knowing that each challenge brought us closer to the life God intended for us. Pressure, far from being a burden, is a gift—a catalyst for miracles and a pathway to purpose.

SKILLS, EXPERIENCE AND KNOWLEDGE

Mature The Mind

A *king and queen* must continuously develop and refine their skills, experience, and knowledge, understanding that ruling a kingdom—or building a family—is a lifelong journey of learning and growth. No ruler starts out perfect; they learn through trials, errors, mistakes, and difficult choices. Each challenge, every setback, and even moments of uncertainty serve as lessons, shaping them into wiser and stronger leaders.

Kathleen and I have experienced this firsthand in raising our family of seven children. There was no manual handed to us—only the willingness to grow, adjust, and commit to becoming better each day. Seeing our children flourish in their own destinies has reinforced our belief that learning never stops. We had to learn how to embrace our role as in-laws and gracefully adjust to the reality of letting our children go as they stepped into marriage, joining their lives with the ones we

SKILLS, EXPERIENCE AND KNOWLEDGE

believe God brought into their paths. And now, as we embrace the role of grandparents, we realize the same truth applies—we must continue to nurture, love, and understand the next generation, just as we did with our own children.

It takes immense skill, experience, and wisdom to nurture a growing family, ensuring that love, unity, and support remain at its core. Just as it takes deep commitment and understanding for a couple to stay together through the years, so too does it require intentionality to keep a family connected as it expands. Learning to release our children with love, trusting in their choices while still being a source of guidance has been one of our greatest lessons—one that continues to shape us as we navigate the evolving dynamics of family, marriage, and generational legacy. We will always be students of life, seeking wisdom, evolving in our knowledge, and ensuring that we not only grow, but truly glow in the journey of love and family.

When Kathleen and I got married, we were young, full of love, and brimming with hope for the future. But like many young couples, we quickly realized that love alone wasn't enough to sustain a lifelong partnership. We lacked the skills, experience, and knowledge that would help us navigate the complexities of marriage, from communication to conflict resolution, finances to parenting. At the time, we relied heavily on what we had observed growing up—what we saw in our parents, grandparents, close friends, and family members. Many of them modeled loving and supportive relationships, and their examples became our foundation. But as we soon discovered, every marriage is unique, and we needed to develop our own skills, gain our own experience, and deepen our own knowledge to thrive as a couple.

Over the years, Kathleen and I have come to understand that skills, experience, and knowledge are not static—they are dynamic, ever-evolving elements of a relationship. They grow as we face challenges, make mistakes, and learn from each other. They are shaped by how we handle situations without creating unnecessary conflict, by how we communicate, and by how we show up for one another. We've learned to appreciate these attributes not just as tools for problem-solving but as gifts that enrich our marriage and help us build a life together.

Drawing from our own journey, Kathleen and I have grown through the years, turning past mistakes into opportunities for growth and using our strengths to build a healthy, balanced partnership.

To understand the importance of skills, experience, and knowledge in marriage, it's helpful to define these concepts:

1. **Skills** are practical abilities that help us navigate specific tasks or challenges. In marriage, skills might include communication, conflict resolution, budgeting, parenting, or time management. These skills can be learned and refined over time, much like mastering a craft.
2. **Experience** refers to the lessons we gain through lived situations. It's the accumulation of moments—both successes and failures—that shape our understanding of what works and what doesn't. Experience teaches us resilience, patience, and adaptability.
3. **Knowledge** is the information and insights we acquire from various sources, including observation, education, and personal growth. In marriage, knowledge might come from books, counseling, spiritual guidance, or learning from other couples. It provides the foundation for making informed decisions and understanding one another.

Together, these three elements form a powerful trio that equips couples to face the challenges of marriage with confidence and grace.

When Kathleen and I first got married, we didn't have a textbook for how to navigate life as a couple. Like many young people, we entered marriage with a mix of expectations, hopes, and misconceptions. We didn't fully understand our roles as husband and

SKILLS, EXPERIENCE AND KNOWLEDGE

wife, nor did we have the skills to handle conflicts without creating tension.

The knowledge we had was shaped by what we had observed growing up. My parents and grandparents modeled hard work, commitment, and the value of standing by your spouse no matter what. Kathleen's family emphasized compassion, generosity, and the importance of emotional connection. These lessons were valuable, but they didn't prepare us for the unique dynamics of our own relationship.

One of the first challenges we faced was learning how to communicate effectively. Kathleen and I quickly realized that our communication styles were different—she tended to approach conversations with emotion, while I leaned toward logic and practicality. This often led to misunderstandings, with both of us feeling unheard or frustrated. It wasn't until we began to actively work on our communication skills—listening without interrupting, expressing our needs clearly, and seeking to understand each other's perspective—that we started to see progress.

Another early challenge was managing our finances. We were young and inexperienced, and like many couples, we struggled to balance our wants and needs. It took time, trial and error, and a lot of patience to develop the budgeting skills that now allow us to plan for the future while meeting our family's needs.

Looking back, those early years were a period of growth. They taught us that skills are not innate—they are learned and cultivated through effort, practice, and a willingness to adapt.

As the king and queen, we each have unique roles and responsibilities, but our goal is the same: to lead our family with love, integrity, and wisdom. Standing as a king and queen requires skills, experience, and knowledge that grow over time.

For me, standing as a king has meant learning how to make decisions with confidence while considering the well-being of our family. It has meant standing up for what I believe in, defending our marriage, and ensuring that Kathleen and our children feel safe and supported.

This role requires practical skills like problem-solving, leadership, and financial planning, as well as emotional intelligence to navigate the nuances of relationships. Kathleen, as the queen, has embraced her role with grace and strength. She fulfills her responsibilities in ways that complement my leadership, often stepping into areas where her strengths shine.

Together, we've learned that being a king and queen is not about hierarchy—it's about partnership. It's about using our skills to support each other, our experience to navigate challenges, and our knowledge to make informed decisions that benefit our family.

Where Do Skills, Experience, and Knowledge Come From?

Skills, experience, and knowledge don't appear out of thin air—they are cultivated through intentional effort and a willingness to learn. Here are some of the sources that have shaped Kathleen and me over the years:

1. **Observation:** Watching other couples, whether in our families or communities, has given us valuable insights into what makes a marriage work. We've learned from both positive examples and cautionary tales, taking note of the behaviours and practices that lead to healthy relationships.
2. **Trial and Error:** Many of our skills and experiences have come from making mistakes and learning from them. Whether it's a financial misstep or a poorly handled argument, each mistake has been an opportunity to grow and improve.
3. **Education:** Reading books, attending workshops, and seeking guidance from mentors have all contributed to our knowledge.

SKILLS, EXPERIENCE AND KNOWLEDGE

Spiritual teachings, in particular, have been a source of wisdom and inspiration, reminding us of the importance of love, respect, and faith in our marriage.
4. **Experience:** Nothing compares to the lessons learned through lived experience. Every challenge we've faced—whether it's raising children, managing a household, or navigating career changes—has added to our reservoir of knowledge and resilience.
5. **God's Guidance:** Above all, we've relied on God to provide the wisdom and strength we need. Through prayer, scripture, and faith, we've found direction and clarity in moments of uncertainty.

Having skills, experience, and knowledge is one thing—using them effectively is another. Kathleen and I have learned that these attributes are only valuable when they are applied with intention and purpose.

Good communication is the foundation of any successful marriage. By using our skills to listen, empathize, and express ourselves clearly, we've built a strong foundation of trust and understanding. Experience has taught us that conflicts are inevitable, but how we handle them makes all the difference. We've learned to approach disagreements with a problem-solving mindset, focusing on solutions rather than blame.

As a team, we use our knowledge to make informed decisions that align with our values and goals. Whether it's financial planning or parenting strategies, we aim to approach decisions with both wisdom and collaboration. We view every challenge as an opportunity to grow. By reflecting on past mistakes and learning from them, we continue to refine our skills and deepen our understanding of each other.

Kathleen and I often say that our mistakes and wrong choices have been some of our greatest teachers. Early in our marriage, we saw these moments as setbacks, but over time, we've come to view them as opportunities for growth. By reflecting on what went wrong and taking steps to improve, we've learned to navigate conflicts with grace and empathy.

Every mistake, no matter how difficult at the time, has been a stepping stone on our journey. Kathleen and I believe that growth comes not from avoiding challenges but from embracing them with a spirit of resilience and determination.

Skills, experience, and knowledge are not destinations—they are part of a lifelong journey. Kathleen and I are still growing, learning, and maturing.

SKILLS, EXPERIENCE AND KNOWLEDGE

COMPLIMENT AND COMPROMISE

The Keys to a Thriving Marriage

A *king and queen* must learn the power of compliment and compromise, recognizing that both are essential for building a deep emotional bond and sustaining unity in leadership. While rulers receive admiration from their people, the most meaningful validation comes from each other—from the words spoken in private moments, from gestures of appreciation that affirm their partnership.

Kathleen and I have come to realize that compliments create emotional security, reinforcing love and trust in ways that cannot be replicated by external praise. I have had many people acknowledge my sermons, teachings, and the life I strive to live as an example, but when Kathleen speaks words of encouragement, it resonates differently—it fills my heart with a sense of fulfillment that no outside approval can match.

COMPLIMENT AND COMPROMISE

Similarly, compromise strengthens our connection, showing us that love is not about winning but about meeting in the middle, finding balance, and choosing unity over personal preference. When we embrace both compliment and compromise, our marriage thrives, drawing us closer emotionally and solidifying the foundation of our love.

Marriage is an intricate dance of two individuals coming together with their unique personalities, values, and experiences. While love and commitment form the foundation, there are two essential ingredients that help sustain a healthy relationship: compliment and compromise. These principles, though simple in concept, hold immense power in building trust, deepening connection, and fostering growth as a couple. However, as Kathleen and I learned early in our marriage, incorporating them into daily life requires intentional effort, understanding, and a willingness to adapt.

Complimenting each other and compromising when necessary are not merely skills; they are acts of kindness and selflessness that reinforce the bond between partners. Sadly, many couples struggle with these practices—whether because of cultural influences, ingrained habits, or personal challenges. Yet, when embraced, compliments and compromise become powerful tools for strengthening relationships, creating harmony, and working together in different roles.

Compliments might seem trivial, but they hold transformative power in relationships. A simple acknowledgment of your spouse's effort, appearance, or contribution can brighten their day, boost their self-esteem, and deepen their sense of connection with you. Unfortunately, many couples overlook the importance of compliments, often withholding them unless explicitly asked. For Kathleen and me, this was a lesson we learned through trial and error, realizing how vital compliments are to fostering a healthy relationship.

When Kathleen and I got married, compliments were not a natural part of my communication. It wasn't that I didn't appreciate her—it simply wasn't part of my cultural upbringing. I grew up in an environment where compliments were rare, reserved for exceptional moments or achievements. This shaped my perspective, leading me to believe that compliments weren't necessary or valuable. Kathleen, however, saw things differently. For her, compliments were an important expression of love and affirmation, a way to connect emotionally and show appreciation.

One of the first challenges we faced was learning to navigate this difference. I vividly remember an instance early in our marriage when Kathleen asked, "How do you like what I'm wearing?" My response, blunt and unfiltered, was, "It doesn't look great on you." I immediately saw the hurt in her eyes and realized my words had done more harm than good. What I should have said was something like, "The blue dress you wore the other day suited you better," offering constructive feedback without being dismissive.

This experience taught me the importance of framing compliments and comments with kindness. Compliments don't have to be extravagant—they simply need to be genuine and thoughtful. When Kathleen puts effort into something, whether it's cooking a meal or choosing an outfit, I make it a point to acknowledge her effort, saying, "You've done a great job with dinner tonight" or "You look beautiful today." These small gestures mean a lot to her, and they've strengthened the emotional intimacy in our relationship.

Compliments are not just about recognizing appearances or actions—they're about valuing the essence of who your partner is. They remind your spouse that they are seen, appreciated, and loved. Kathleen and I have learned that compliments don't cost anything, yet their impact is priceless. They create positivity, encourage growth, and reinforce the bond that holds a marriage together.

COMPLIMENT AND COMPROMISE

Despite their importance, compliments are often neglected in relationships. Some people believe compliments are unnecessary, thinking their spouse should already know they are valued. Others see them as awkward or insincere, especially if they weren't raised in an environment where compliments were common. Cultural influences, personal beliefs, and long-standing habits can all contribute to this dynamic.

For Kathleen and me, cultural differences played a significant role. Compliments were part of Kathleen's nature, shaped by her upbringing in a family that valued emotional connection. For me, they were foreign, an idea that required conscious effort to incorporate into our marriage. Learning to give compliments wasn't easy—it felt unnatural at first—but over time, I saw how much they meant to Kathleen and how they positively influenced our relationship.

Another reason couples overlook compliments is the misconception that they become irrelevant after years of marriage. This belief often leads to stagnation, with partners forgetting to celebrate each other's efforts or achievements. Kathleen and I have made it a priority to avoid this pitfall, ensuring that compliments remain an active part of our communication, no matter how long we've been together.

While compliments add warmth to a relationship, compromise is the glue that holds it together. Marriage is not about "me, myself, and I"—it's about "we and us." Compromise requires setting aside personal preferences, adjusting habits, and finding solutions that benefit both partners. It's a practice of humility, empathy, and collaboration, and though it can be challenging, it is essential for a healthy and balanced partnership.

For Kathleen and me, compromise was a difficult concept to embrace, especially in the early years of our marriage. As someone who left home at 17 and worked hard to establish my independence, I was used to making decisions on my own without consulting anyone. By the time I met Kathleen, I had already developed my own way of doing things, shaped by my extroverted, bold, and enthusiastic nature. Compromise, for me, felt like relinquishing control, something I struggled with deeply.

Kathleen, however, approached compromise with a sense of ease. Her introverted and adaptable personality made her more willing to go with the flow, adjusting to situations without resistance. This difference between us created tension at times, especially when I resisted making changes to my habits or expectations. But over time, I realized that compromise wasn't about losing my identity—it was about creating space for Kathleen's needs and perspectives.

One area where compromise became particularly important was in our decision-making. As an extrovert, I often wanted to take charge and make quick decisions, while Kathleen preferred to reflect and take her time. This contrast occasionally led to disagreements, but as we learned to compromise, we found ways to balance our approaches. I started to slow down and consider Kathleen's insights, while she became more comfortable with spontaneity and action. Together, we created a rhythm that honoured both of our styles.

Compromise also plays a crucial role in addressing conflicts. Kathleen and I have learned that conflicts are not about winning or proving who's right—they're about finding solutions that strengthen the relationship. By focusing on the issue at hand and approaching it collaboratively, we've developed a practice of compromise that helps us navigate disagreements with respect and empathy.

Compromise is not always easy, especially for couples who marry later in life or have established habits and routines. The longer we live independently, the harder it becomes to adjust our behaviours and expectations. Kathleen and I experienced this firsthand, with both of us bringing our own preferences and beliefs into the relationship.

COMPLIMENT AND COMPROMISE

For me, compromise felt like surrender. I was used to standing my ground, defending my choices, and pursuing my goals without interference. Kathleen's adaptable nature, while helpful, often made me feel like I needed to lead the way. It took time and reflection to recognize that compromise isn't a weakness—it's a strength. It's a practice of valuing your partner's voice and working together to build a partnership that benefits both of you.

Kathleen, on the other hand, had to learn to assert herself in moments when compromise was needed. Her natural inclination to "go with the flow" sometimes left her feeling unheard or unacknowledged. As we grew together, she found her voice, learning to express her needs and perspectives with confidence. This growth has been a beautiful testament to the power of compromise in creating equality and balance in a relationship.

Compliment and compromise are not isolated practices—they are deeply interconnected. Compliments create positivity and encouragement, while compromise fosters collaboration and unity. Together, they form the foundation of a healthy relationship, helping couples navigate challenges with grace and teamwork.

For Kathleen and me, these practices have strengthened our bond in countless ways. Compliments remind us to celebrate each other's contributions, while compromise teaches us to value each other's perspectives. When we approach decisions or conflicts, we do so with mutual respect, knowing that our marriage is built on a commitment to support and uplift one another.

One example of how these principles intersect is in our parenting journey. Raising seven children requires constant collaboration, from managing schedules to addressing challenges. Kathleen's nurturing approach complements my logical style, and through compromise, we've found ways to integrate both perspectives. Compliments keep us motivated, reminding us to acknowledge each other's efforts and celebrate small victories.

Practical Steps for Incorporating Compliment and Compromise

Couples who want to strengthen their relationship through compliment and compromise can start with these practical steps:

1. **Make Compliments a Habit:** Incorporate compliments into your daily interactions, whether it's acknowledging your spouse's effort, appearance, or contribution. Be sincere and specific to make your compliments meaningful.
2. **Practice Constructive Feedback:** When offering feedback, frame your words positively to avoid causing hurt. Instead of criticizing, focus on highlighting what works and offering suggestions.
3. **Value Your Partner's Perspective:** Compromise starts with empathy. Seek to understand your partner's needs and preferences, and work together to find solutions that benefit both of you.
4. **Communicate Openly:** Share your thoughts and feelings honestly, creating a safe space for dialogue. Effective communication strengthens both compliment and compromise.
5. **Celebrate Successes Together:** Whether it's a small achievement or a major milestone, take time to celebrate each other's efforts and growth.

COMPLIMENT AND COMPROMISE

AVOID PROBLEMS DOMINATING

Let Love Rule

We need to avoid problems from dominating our lives, because when difficulties are allowed to take center stage, they can slowly drain the love, unity, and peace from a marriage. A *king and queen* must learn this principle, knowing that if they see each other as the problem rather than working together to confront the challenge, their kingdom will divide.

Kathleen and I have had to remind ourselves time and time again that while problems may come—whether financial struggles, addiction, behavioural differences, or personality conflicts—the true test is how we handle them. Taking responsibility for our actions when we make mistakes is necessary, but at the same time, we must see each other as God's masterpiece, rather than allowing difficulties to overshadow the love we share.

AVOID PROBLEMS DOMINATING

Problems are like leeches—they can drain the life out of a marriage if we let them. The only way we have kept love ruling in our lives is by choosing not to let issues dominate our emotions, refusing to let frustration lead us to hurt each other with words or actions. When love takes priority, problems lose their power, and healing begins.

In every relationship, problems are inevitable. Life is unpredictable, and challenges will always surface—whether it's financial struggles, intimacy issues, communication barriers, or emotional pain rooted in past mistakes. These issues, if left unchecked, have the potential to overshadow love, making it secondary to the problems at hand.

Kathleen and I learned this lesson early in our marriage. There were times when our focus on the problems we faced caused the love we shared to feel distant, like a dim light struggling to shine through the fog of challenges. The emotional bond that once felt so strong began to weaken under the weight of the issues that dominated our relationship.

But through reflection, intentional effort, and a commitment to prioritizing love, we discovered that it's possible to shift the balance. Problems don't have to dominate a marriage; love can take the lead. Just like a coffee cup full of black coffee can be transformed into clear water when placed under a running tap, so too can love wash away the residue of problems when it is allowed to flow freely. This process requires deliberate action—a conscious decision to renew love, prioritize emotional connection, and create space for growth and healing.

Couples can avoid letting problems dominate their relationships. Drawing from our own journey, we have developed insights and practical steps for renewing love, addressing challenges, and keeping the emotional bond alive even in the face of adversity.

When problems dominate a relationship, they act like a cloud that obscures the light of love. Kathleen and I have experienced this firsthand. There were times when financial stress consumed our thoughts, leaving little room for laughter, connection, or intimacy.

Instead of enjoying each other's company, we found ourselves discussing bills, budgets, and expenses at every turn. The love we shared felt like it was being pushed into the background, overshadowed by the constant weight of our challenges.

The problem with allowing issues to dominate is that they become all-consuming. They shape how you see your partner, your relationship, and even yourself. The more you focus on the problem, the more it grows, creating distance between you and your spouse. Instead of working as a team to address the challenge, it's easy to fall into a pattern of blame, frustration, and disconnection.

One important lessons Kathleen and I learned is that problems are not the enemy—how we approach them is what makes the difference. By shifting our perspective and prioritizing love, we were able to break free from the cycle of negativity and restore the emotional bond that is the foundation of our marriage.

The analogy of a coffee cup full of black coffee being transformed into clear water under a running tap perfectly illustrates how love can flush out the dominance of problems. Just as the flow of water gradually replaces the coffee, so too can an intentional flow of love and positivity replace the weight of challenges in a relationship.

For Kathleen and me, this meant making a deliberate effort to bring love back into the center of our marriage. We realized that if we wanted our relationship to thrive, we needed to nurture our connection and create an environment where love could flourish. This didn't mean ignoring our problems—it meant addressing them in a way that prioritized our emotional bond.

We started by setting aside time each week to focus solely on each other. Whether it was a date night, a walk in the park, or simply sitting together to talk about our dreams and goals, these moments allowed us to reconnect and remind ourselves of why we fell in love in the first place. We also made it a point to express appreciation for one another,

AVOID PROBLEMS DOMINATING

celebrating the small acts of kindness and support that often go unnoticed.

By allowing love to flow freely in our relationship, we found that problems began to lose their grip. They no longer felt insurmountable because we were tackling them as a team, united by the strength of our bond.

Just like you can train your non-dominant hand to become stronger with practice, you can also train love to dominate a relationship, even when problems try to take center stage. Renewing the "first love" honeymoon feeling isn't about recreating the past—it's about reigniting the passion, connection, and joy that brought you together.

For Kathleen and me, this process required intentional effort. Over time, we had fallen into routines that prioritized responsibilities over romance, and we needed to find ways to bring spontaneity and excitement back into our relationship. Here are some of the steps we took:

1. **Revisit the Early Days:** We spent time reminiscing about our courtship, sharing stories about our favorite memories and what initially drew us to each other. This helped us reconnect with the feelings of love and admiration that first sparked our relationship.
2. **Practice Gratitude:** Gratitude became a cornerstone of our relationship. Each day, we made it a habit to express one thing we were grateful for about each other. This simple practice shifted our focus from the problems we faced to the blessings we shared.
3. **Prioritize Intimacy:** Physical and emotional intimacy are essential for maintaining a strong connection. Whether it was holding hands, sharing a heartfelt conversation, or spending quality time together, we made intimacy a priority in our marriage.

4. **Celebrate Small Victories:** Even in the midst of challenges, we found reasons to celebrate. Whether it was achieving a financial goal or simply making it through a tough week, these moments of celebration reminded us of our resilience and the strength of our partnership.

Renewing love takes practice and effort, but the rewards are well worth it. By making love the dominant force in your relationship, you create a foundation that can withstand even the toughest challenges.

While every relationship is unique, there are common issues that often take over if left unchecked. Kathleen and I have faced many of these challenges, and we've learned that addressing them head-on is essential for maintaining a healthy relationship.

Money is one of the leading causes of tension in relationships. Whether it's managing debt, budgeting, or planning for the future, financial stress can quickly overshadow love if not addressed.

Physical and emotional intimacy are vital for a healthy relationship, but they can be affected by stress, fatigue, or unresolved conflicts.

Misunderstandings, lack of active listening, and poor communication habits can create distance and frustration between partners.

Past mistakes, dishonesty, or unmet expectations can erode trust, making it difficult to maintain a strong emotional bond.

Struggles with addiction or abusive behaviours can have a profound impact on a relationship, requiring professional support and intervention.

Holding onto resentment or revisiting past mistakes can prevent a relationship from moving forward.

AVOID PROBLEMS DOMINATING

Addressing these issues with love, empathy, and teamwork is key to preventing them from dominating a relationship. Kathleen and I have found that by tackling challenges together, we can turn even the most difficult situations into opportunities for growth and connection.

One of the most powerful ways to keep love at the forefront of a relationship is to renew the "honeymoon feeling." This doesn't mean pretending that challenges don't exist—it means making a conscious effort to nurture the joy, excitement, and passion that brought you together.

Kathleen and I have embraced this practice throughout our marriage. Whether it's surprising each other with small acts of kindness, taking time to laugh and have fun, or simply being present in the moment, we've learned that love thrives when it's given the attention it deserves.

Renewing the honeymoon feeling also involves letting go of the past. Resentment, regret, and unresolved conflicts can weigh heavily on a relationship, making it difficult to move forward. By choosing forgiveness and focusing on the present, couples can create a space where love can flourish.

Problems are inevitable in any relationship, but they don't have to define it. Kathleen and I have learned that by prioritizing love, addressing challenges as a team, and renewing our emotional bond, we can prevent problems from taking over.

Love is a powerful force—it has the ability to heal, to connect, and to overcome even the greatest obstacles. By allowing love to flow freely in your relationship, you can flush out the problems that threaten to dominate, creating a partnership that is resilient, joyful, and enduring.

As Kathleen and I continue our journey together, we remain committed to choosing love over problems, trusting that this choice will sustain us through every season of life.

YOUR PROBLEM YOUR ISSUE

Don't Let You Problem Be My Issue

A *king and queen* must learn that their personal struggles should not become their spouse's burden, especially when those struggles stem from unmet expectations. If the king holds certain desires that go unfulfilled, that is his issue to process, not the queen's weight to carry. Likewise, if the queen has expectations that are not met, she must recognize that her personal disappointment is not something to place on the king's shoulders.

Kathleen and I have come to understand that problems arise when we try to make each other into a reflection of ourselves—forcing our ways, perspectives, or desires onto the other instead of appreciating who we are individually. The king cannot mould his queen into a replica of himself, nor can the queen reshape the king into her likeness.

Growth happens when each person takes ownership of their emotions, challenges, and needs, without demanding their spouse carry their burdens as their own. This lesson took years for Kathleen and me to master, and once we did, it removed unnecessary arguments, strengthened our communication, and allowed us to love each other more freely—with acceptance instead of expectation.

Marriage is a partnership—a dynamic union of two individuals with their own thoughts, feelings, and challenges. While this partnership is built on mutual love and support, it's easy to fall into a pattern where personal problems begin to bleed into the relationship, turning them into the other spouse's issue. Kathleen and I have encountered this challenge many times throughout our marriage. It's human nature to externalize frustrations, to want someone else to share in our burdens. But over time, we've come to understand that allowing personal problems to dominate the relationship can erode the emotional bond and create unnecessary tension.

This doesn't mean we face our struggles alone. Instead, Kathleen and I have learned that there's a difference between asking for support and projecting a personal problem onto your spouse. The key is taking responsibility for your own challenges and approaching them constructively, rather than letting them dictate the dynamics of your marriage.

One of the first things Kathleen and I learned in our marriage is how easy it is to externalize personal problems. When something bothers us—whether it's a bad day at work, household chores left undone, or unmet expectations—it's tempting to direct that frustration at the nearest target: your spouse.

There were times when I'd come home to find dirty dishes piled up in the sink. My immediate reaction was frustration, and my instinct was to let Kathleen know exactly how I felt about it. I'd think to myself, "Why aren't these dishes cleaned? I've had a long day, and the least I could come home to is a tidy kitchen." I would never put thought that she may have had a bad day, busy with the children, doing other chores etc. But as I let those thoughts simmer, I realized something important:

the dirty dishes weren't Kathleen's problem—they were mine. They bothered *me*. If they weren't addressed in the way I wanted them to be, it was my responsibility to take action—not to make Kathleen feel guilty or inadequate.

Instead of allowing my frustration to spill over into our relationship, I learned to address the issue calmly. If I noticed the dishes and they bothered me, I started simply cleaning them myself. This didn't mean I avoided talking about it with Kathleen—it meant I reframed my approach. Rather than yelling, getting upset, or assigning blame, I initiated a respectful conversation. This approach shifted the dynamic from conflict to collaboration, helping us tackle the root cause without damaging our bond. After considering this happens a few times and not all the time, that also had to be considered to avoid conflict.

One important lessons Kathleen and I have learned is that yelling, screaming, and getting angry rarely, if ever, leads to a productive resolution. Emotional outbursts may provide a temporary release for the person expressing their frustration, but they often leave the other person feeling defensive, hurt, or disengaged. When this cycle repeats, it can create a toxic environment where communication breaks down and problems remain unresolved.

Instead of resorting to anger, Kathleen and I made it a point to focus on addressing concerns calmly and constructively. For example, if one of us had an issue, we'd take a step back and ask ourselves: *What is the root cause of this problem? Is it really about my spouse, or is it something I need to address within myself?* This self-reflection often revealed that the frustration wasn't about the other person—it was about unmet expectations, internal stress, or a need for better communication.

When we did talk about our concerns, we used "I" statements to express how we felt without placing blame. For instance, instead of saying, "You never help with the dishes," I'd say, "I feel overwhelmed when there are dishes left in the sink after a long day. Can we work together to come up with a solution?" This approach invited collaboration rather than conflict, allowing us to work through the issue as a team.

One of the cornerstones of avoiding the "your problem becomes my issue" trap is personal accountability. Taking responsibility for your own feelings, reactions, and challenges is crucial for maintaining a healthy relationship. It's easy to fall into the mindset of expecting your spouse to "fix" your problems or alleviate your frustrations, but this places an unfair burden on the other person and can create resentment over time.

Kathleen and I have made it a habit to remind ourselves that we are each responsible for our own emotions and reactions. This doesn't mean we don't rely on each other for support—it means we approach our struggles with self-awareness and a willingness to do the internal work needed to address them. For instance, if I'm feeling stressed or frustrated, I take a moment to assess why I'm feeling that way before bringing it into our relationship. This self-reflection helps me communicate my needs more effectively and prevents me from projecting my emotions onto Kathleen.

Accountability also means being willing to take action to resolve problems rather than expecting your spouse to do it for you. If something bothers me—whether it's the state of the house, a financial concern, or a work-related issue—I ask myself, *What can I do to address this?* By taking ownership of my role in the situation, I can approach Kathleen with solutions rather than complaints, creating a more positive and productive dynamic.

Kathleen and I have walked through many challenges, especially in the earlier years of our marriage, that other couples can likely relate to. These struggles often arise as couples transition from individual lives to a shared union. Early in our marriage, we struggled to find the right balance between spending time together as a couple and maintaining individual interests and friendships. As newlyweds, we often felt guilty for needing personal space, which sometimes led to feelings of neglect or misunderstanding.

Many couples face the tension of wanting to nurture the relationship without losing their sense of individuality. Over time, we learned that having personal time isn't selfish—it's necessary for emotional health.

Determining who would handle what tasks around the house was initially a source of frustration. Kathleen might have assumed I'd automatically help with certain chores, while I thought differently based on how I was raised. For example, she took charge of meal preparation, but I assumed handling repairs and finances was enough to contribute. This sometimes left her feeling overwhelmed and unacknowledged. Many couples experience these unspoken expectations based on their upbringing. Without clear communication, it's easy for resentment to build when one partner feels the responsibilities are unevenly distributed.

My natural tendency to communicate logically often clashed with Kathleen's more emotionally driven style. Early disagreements would escalate because I was trying to "fix" the situation with a solution, while Kathleen simply wanted to feel heard. Communication misunderstandings are a major source of tension for couples. Adjusting to each other's needs—whether that's active listening or finding the right time to address issues—can take significant effort.

Kathleen and I had different ways of interacting with our families, and there were moments when differing levels of involvement or expectations from our families created stress. For example, one side might expect us to spend more time with them during holidays, which created difficult choices. Many couples face tension when trying to balance their relationship with external family expectations. Setting healthy boundaries while honouring family ties is essential but often challenging in the early years.

YOUR PROBLEM YOUR ISSUE

When we had children, we realized we had slightly different ideas about parenting. Kathleen leaned toward nurturing and emotional support, while I emphasized structure and discipline. These differences led to some disagreements about how to handle parenting challenges. Parenting introduces a new set of challenges for couples, especially when differing approaches need to be reconciled. It can take time to align as a parenting team.

Early in our marriage, balancing my career aspirations and Kathleen's personal goals was a juggling act. There were times when my long work hours clashed with Kathleen's need for quality time, leading to feelings of imbalance in our priorities. Many couples struggle to align career aspirations with relationship needs, especially when one partner feels overlooked or unsupported during busy seasons.

When disagreements arose, Kathleen sometimes held onto the frustration longer than necessary, while I preferred to address and move past issues more quickly. This dynamic occasionally created tension when one of us felt like the conflict wasn't fully resolved. Forgiveness is a cornerstone of a healthy relationship, but it can be challenging in the early years when couples are still learning to navigate conflict effectively.

In the early years, physical intimacy sometimes became an area of miscommunication. I may have had different expectations compared to Kathleen, and we had to learn to discuss and compromise in this area without making assumptions. Many couples struggle with aligning expectations when it comes to intimacy. Open and honest conversations are essential for fostering trust and connection.

During high-stress situations—whether it was juggling finances, raising children, or dealing with external pressures—we sometimes struggled to support each other effectively. My instinct was to problem-solve, while Kathleen needed emotional support and reassurance. Stress can easily magnify small issues in a relationship, making it important for couples to recognize how they can best support each other during tough times.

These examples from our early years of marriage illustrate that every relationship comes with its own set of challenges. While each couple's journey is unique, the principles of communication, empathy, compromise, and teamwork are universal. Kathleen and I have learned that challenges are not signs of failure—they are opportunities to grow stronger together. Facing these issues with love and intentionality has not only deepened our connection but also given us the tools to navigate life's ups and downs with grace and resilience.

One transformative shifts in our relationship has been learning to separate the problem from the person. It's easy to conflate the two, especially when emotions are running high. But blaming your spouse for a problem only creates distance and conflict. Instead, Kathleen and I have learned to focus on the issue itself, working together to find a resolution without assigning blame.

If there's a recurring issue—like household chores not being evenly distributed—we approach it as a shared challenge rather than a personal failure. We ask questions like, "How can we make this easier for both of us?" or "What changes can we implement to address this?" This mindset creates a sense of partnership and encourages open communication.

Separating the problem from the person also requires empathy. Kathleen and I make an effort to understand each other's perspectives and needs, even when we don't necessarily agree. This empathy allows us to approach problems with compassion and a shared commitment to finding solutions that work for both of us.

One of the risks of letting your personal problem become your spouse's issue is the potential for emotional overflow. When we don't address our own challenges, they can spill over into the relationship, creating unnecessary tension and conflict. Kathleen and I have experienced this dynamic, particularly during stressful seasons when external pressures—like work, finances, or parenting—felt overwhelming.

To avoid emotional overflow, we've learned the importance of self-regulation. This means taking time to process our own emotions before bringing them into the relationship. Whether it's going for a walk, journaling, praying, or simply taking a few deep breaths, these practices help us approach our spouse with a clear mind and a calm heart.

We've also made it a priority to establish boundaries around stressors. For example, if one of us is dealing with a work-related issue, we communicate our needs clearly: "I've had a tough day at work, and I need a little time to decompress before we talk." This transparency allows us to support each other without feeling overwhelmed by the other person's challenges.

Practical Strategies for Avoiding Projection

Avoiding the tendency to make your problem your spouse's issue requires intentional effort and practical strategies. Here are some of the practices that have helped Kathleen and me navigate this dynamic:

1. **Identify the Root Cause:** Before addressing a problem with your spouse, take time to reflect on the underlying cause of your frustration. Ask yourself, *Is this really about them, or is it about me?*
2. **Communicate With Clarity:** Use "I" statements to express your feelings and needs without assigning blame. For example, "I feel stressed when the house is messy. Can we come up with a plan to keep things organized?"
3. **Take Ownership:** If something bothers you, take responsibility for addressing it rather than expecting your spouse to fix it. This doesn't mean you can't ask for support—it means approaching the issue with accountability.

4. **Create Space for Dialogue:** Set aside time to discuss recurring issues in a calm and constructive manner. Focus on finding solutions together rather than placing blame.
5. **Practice Empathy:** Try to see the situation from your spouse's perspective. Understanding their feelings and needs can help you approach challenges with compassion and collaboration.
6. **Manage Stress Effectively:** Develop healthy coping strategies for managing stress and processing emotions. This will prevent personal challenges from spilling over into the relationship.

Kathleen and I's journey of avoiding the "your problem becomes my issue" trap has been one of growth, self-awareness, and mutual respect. We've learned that while marriage is a partnership, it's also a union of two individuals who must take responsibility for their own challenges. By approaching problems constructively, separating the issue from the person, and prioritizing accountability, we've been able to create a relationship that is both supportive and balanced.

Marriage is not about blaming your spouse for your struggles—it's about working together to navigate life's challenges with empathy, love, and grace. As Kathleen and I continue to grow in our relationship, we remain committed to fostering a partnership where problems are addressed without overshadowing the love and connection we share.

YOUR PROBLEM YOUR ISSUE

THE EGGSHELL ENVIRONMENT

Strengthening Emotional Bonds

Can you imagine the eggshell environment that would be created in a kingdom where the *king and queen* are constantly at odds—fighting, arguing, and refusing to stand together? A divided leadership leads to a fragile foundation, causing tension, uncertainty, and instability for everyone under their rule.

Kathleen and I have learned that when conflict lingers unchecked, it weakens us as a cuple and slowly erodes the trust and connection we have worked so hard to build. Just as a kingdom cannot thrive under divided leadership, marriage cannot flourish when partners allow disagreements to pull them apart instead of finding ways to stand strong together. The only way to truly rule as a king and queen is to commit to unity, refusing to let frustration, misunderstandings, or external pressures create distance. There is power in standing together, in prioritizing love over conflict, and in remembering that no disagreement should ever be greater than the bond we share. A king and queen who

THE EGGSHELL ENVIRONMENT

recognize this protect their kingdom—just as a husband and wife must protect their marriage.

Relationships are meant to be a place of comfort, trust, and love—a sanctuary where partners feel safe and valued. But when disagreements and arguments arise, it's easy to fall into what Kathleen and I call the "eggshell environment," where tension is so thick that communication feels strained and walking on eggshells becomes the norm.

Early in our marriage, we learned that retreating into emotional distance—whether by sleeping in separate beds, staying with friends or family, or turning cold shoulders—only served to weaken our connection. While it may seem like an escape in the moment, this behaviour can jeopardize the years of investment in building a strong emotional bond.

Through trial and error, we learned the importance of breaking free from the eggshell environment and choosing resolution over resentment. Facing disagreements with grace, open communication, and intentional problem-solving not only helped us grow as a couple but also strengthened the foundation of trust that keeps a relationship thriving. In this chapter, I'll explore strategies to avoid the eggshell environment, share personal insights from our journey, and offer practical tools for creating a relationship where love dominates even during times of conflict.

Living in an eggshell environment comes with steep emotional costs. Kathleen and I discovered that when tension lingers after disagreements, it doesn't just create awkwardness—it starts to erode the intimacy and trust we worked so hard to build. In the early years of our marriage, there were times when we'd argue about finances, parenting, or household responsibilities, and instead of resolving the conflict, we'd retreat into silence. I would withdraw, convinced that time apart would cool things down, while Kathleen—hurt and frustrated—would let the distance deepen.

This behaviour led to patterns that were destructive. Sleeping in separate rooms, going to bed without speaking, and taking "space" without constructive communication didn't fix the problems; it simply made them harder to address. The unresolved tension began to weigh heavily on our relationship, creating emotional walls that were difficult to break down.

What Kathleen and I eventually realized is that the eggshell environment doesn't just delay resolution—it actively undermines the love that binds two people together. Avoiding conflict doesn't erase it; it amplifies it. Problems fester, emotions simmer, and the bond that holds a relationship together starts to weaken. Breaking free from this cycle requires intentional effort and a willingness to confront issues directly.

One of the lessons Kathleen and I learned is the value of talking it out. Open and honest communication is the antidote to the eggshell environment. While it's tempting to avoid difficult conversations, addressing disagreements head-on prevents them from turning into long-standing issues.

For us, learning to communicate effectively took time. Early on, I had a tendency to "jump out" during heated moments, letting frustration guide my words instead of pausing to listen. Kathleen, on the other hand, sometimes found it hard to express her feelings, fearing that she might escalate the situation or be misunderstood. These dynamics created tension that made resolution difficult.

What helped us was adopting a few key practices that transformed the way we approached communication:

1. **Listen Without Interrupting:** Active listening became our cornerstone. We made it a priority to hear each other out fully before responding, even if we didn't initially agree with what was being said.

THE EGGSHELL ENVIRONMENT

2. **Avoid Jumping to Conclusions:** Instead of assuming the worst or jumping to defend ourselves, we learned to ask clarifying questions. This allowed us to understand each other's perspectives without turning the conversation into a debate.
3. **Speak With Respect:** Using "I" statements to express feelings and concerns helped us avoid assigning blame. For example, saying "I feel hurt when…" instead of "You always…" kept the conversation constructive.
4. **Set a Calm Tone:** Before diving into difficult conversations, we made an effort to approach them calmly. If emotions were running high, we'd take a moment to breathe and reflect before engaging.

These practices helped us turn conflict into collaboration, teaching us that communication is not just about solving problems—it's about strengthening the connection between partners.

One harmful aspects of the eggshell environment is the tendency to take disagreements personally. Kathleen and I struggled with this early in our marriage, particularly when our arguments touched on sensitive topics like money or parenting. It's easy to feel targeted when your spouse voices concerns, but what we learned is that the problem is rarely about the person—it's about the issue itself.

For example, if Kathleen raised concerns about our spending habits, I initially felt defensive, as if she were criticizing me. In reality, her concerns weren't an attack—they were an effort to address a problem that affected both of us. Similarly, when I brought up parenting decisions, Kathleen sometimes felt like I was questioning her abilities. But as we talked things out, we realized that neither of us was trying to hurt the other—we were simply trying to navigate challenges as a team.

Separating the problem from the person requires empathy and a willingness to see things from your spouse's perspective. Kathleen and I learned to approach conflicts with questions like:

- "What's really bothering you about this situation?"
- "How can we work together to address this issue?"
- "What's the best solution for both of us?"

These questions helped us shift the focus from blame to problem-solving, creating a space where discussions could lead to resolution rather than resentment.

Not all disagreements can be solved immediately, and sometimes the best approach is to let the dust settle before addressing the issue. Kathleen and I learned that taking a moment to cool off—without retreating into silence or emotional distance—can be a powerful way to avoid impulsive reactions.

For example, if a disagreement escalated and emotions were running high, we'd agree to step away temporarily. Instead of storming off or shutting down, we'd communicate our intentions: "I need a little time to gather my thoughts, but let's revisit this conversation soon." This approach allowed us to process our feelings while keeping the door open for resolution.

Timing is crucial when it comes to addressing conflicts. Tackling an issue when emotions are raw often leads to reactive arguments rather than productive discussions. Kathleen and I found that taking a step back, reflecting on the situation, and approaching it with clarity made all the difference.

The eggshell environment often stems from behaviours like emotional bullying or impulsive reactions—things Kathleen and I both struggled with at times. Emotional bullying, whether intentional or unintentional, creates a dynamic where one partner feels intimidated or manipulated during disagreements. Impulsive reactions, on the other hand, amplify tension and make resolution harder to achieve.

To break free from these patterns, Kathleen and I committed to practicing self-awareness and emotional regulation. This meant:

THE EGGSHELL ENVIRONMENT

- **Recognizing Triggers:** Understanding what sets off reactive behaviours allowed us to address them proactively.
- **Pausing Before Responding:** Taking a moment to breathe and think before speaking helped us avoid saying things we'd regret.
- **Respecting Boundaries:** We made it a point to avoid pushing each other during heated moments, ensuring that discussions remained respectful.

By avoiding these behaviours, we created an environment where both of us felt safe to express ourselves without fear of judgment or retaliation.

Avoiding the eggshell environment requires both partners to take on this mindset, standing together as equals fighting for the same goal: a thriving relationship.

As king and queen, we learned to balance strength with humility, recognizing that disagreements are not battles to be won but opportunities to grow. By approaching conflicts with the intention to resolve rather than dominate, we've been able to build a partnership that values mutual respect and teamwork.

Here are some practical strategies that have helped Kathleen and me break free from the eggshell environment:

1. **Don't Go to Bed Angry:** Make it a priority to address disagreements before the day ends. Even if the issue isn't fully resolved, expressing love and a commitment to work through it can prevent emotional distance.
2. **Create a Safe Space for Discussions:** Establish ground rules for how disagreements will be handled—no yelling, no blaming, and a commitment to listening actively.
3. **Take Ownership of Your Actions:** Acknowledge your role in the disagreement and be willing to apologize when necessary. Accountability is key to rebuilding trust.

4. **Separate the Problem From the Person:** Focus on the issue at hand rather than making personal attacks. Approach disagreements as a team, working together to find solutions.
5. **Prioritize Love Over Conflict:** Even during challenging moments, remind each other of your love and commitment. Small gestures, like holding hands or sharing a kind word, can help defuse tension.

Avoiding the eggshell environment is not about avoiding conflict—it's about choosing unity over tension, resolution over resentment, and love over distance. Kathleen and I have learned that disagreements are a natural part of any relationship, but how we handle them defines the strength of our bond.

By practicing open communication, letting the dust settle, avoiding emotional bullying, and standing together as partners, we've been able to create a relationship that thrives even during challenging moments. Love is the foundation of our marriage, and we remain committed to nurturing it with every step of our journey.

THE EGGSHELL ENVIRONMENT

AVOID EMOTIONAL BULLYING

Is The Fighting Worth The Casulity

In order to *stand as a king and rule as a queen*, they had to ask themselves, "Is the fighting worth the casualty?" Every disagreement carries the potential to either strengthen or weaken the kingdom, and wise rulers know that some battles simply aren't worth the damage they can cause.

Kathleen and I had to learn this truth in our marriage—we had to be intentional about choosing which discussions truly mattered, instead of letting minor frustrations turn into unnecessary conflicts. One of the most important lessons we embraced was the need to avoid emotional bullying—never using words to wound, never allowing frustration to become a weapon against each other.

Over time, we realized that picking at each other for every small thing only drained the love and connection we worked so hard to build. Instead, we focused on respectful discussions that lead to growth, keeping our kingdom strong by prioritizing unity over the desire to always be "right." Marriage is not about winning arguments—it's about winning in love, trust, and mutual respect.

One concepts Kathleen and I learned early in our marriage is that fighting, in any form—whether verbal, physical, or emotional—is never worth the damage it causes to a relationship. The idea of fighting might seem like a natural reaction to disagreements or frustrations, but in the context of a loving partnership, it often leads to outcomes that are more destructive than constructive. Yelling, giving each other the cold shoulder, walking away, or venting to friends or family doesn't solve the problem—it only magnifies the distance between two people who are supposed to be fighting *for* each other, not *against* each other.

Kathleen and I weren't immune to the temptation to lash out during the early stages of our marriage. We found ourselves caught in the trap of using emotion, frustration, or silence as weapons during disagreements. These moments taught us an important truth: fighting—no matter how justified it may feel in the moment—is not worth sacrificing the love, respect, and emotional bond we share. Over time, we learned to prioritize resolution over conflict, choosing constructive communication and mutual understanding as the foundation for navigating challenges. By choosing love over anger, couples can build a partnership that thrives on trust, respect, and resilience.

Like many couples, Kathleen and I entered marriage with a mix of love, excitement, and naivety about what it really takes to build a life together. We were committed to each other but still learning how to navigate the complexities of sharing a life. Early disagreements often escalated into arguments, fueled by misunderstandings, unmet expectations, and the stress of adjusting to new roles.

There was a time when we argued about everything, it was like neither one of us can do anything right without being criticized—a common source of tension for newlyweds. I approached the issue with frustration, letting my emotions dictate my words, while Kathleen retreated into silence, hurt by the way I expressed my concerns. This dynamic created a cycle of conflict where neither of us felt heard or validated. Instead of addressing the issue constructively, we allowed the disagreement to morph into a war of words and feelings, leaving both of us drained and disconnected.

These moments taught us that fighting, even when it feels justified, is never worth the casualty it creates in the relationship. Every angry word, cold shoulder, or unresolved argument chips away at the emotional bond we worked so hard to build. What we needed wasn't more conflict—it was a way to navigate our differences without causing harm.

Fighting, in any form, comes with significant emotional and relational costs. Kathleen and I experienced firsthand how unresolved conflicts can lead to feelings of resentment, mistrust, and emotional distance. Here are some of the ways fighting can negatively impact a relationship:

1. **Erosion of Trust:** When arguments escalate into verbal attacks or emotional withdrawal, trust begins to erode. Couples may start to question whether their partner truly respects or values them, leading to feelings of insecurity.
2. **Emotional Burnout:** Constant fighting takes an emotional toll on both partners, leaving them feeling exhausted, drained, and disconnected. This burnout can make it harder to approach future conflicts with clarity and patience.
3. **Breakdown of Communication:** Fighting often disrupts effective communication, replacing dialogue with defensiveness and blame. Instead of resolving the issue, partners may find themselves stuck in a cycle of miscommunication.
4. **Damage to Intimacy:** Emotional intimacy thrives on connection and vulnerability, but fighting can create walls that

AVOID EMOTIONAL BULLYING

prevent partners from feeling close or supported. Over time, this can lead to feelings of loneliness within the relationship.

5. **Reinforcement of Negative Patterns:** When fighting becomes a habitual response to disagreements, it reinforces negative patterns of behaviour that are difficult to break.

Kathleen and I realized that the consequences of fighting were not worth the temporary release of frustration. What mattered more was finding ways to address our differences constructively, preserving the love and respect we shared.

One of the most important changes Kathleen and I made in our relationship was shifting our focus from fighting to resolution. We learned that disagreements don't have to turn into battles—they can be opportunities for growth and understanding.

Here are some of the strategies that helped us make this shift:

1. **Pause Before Reacting:** When tensions rise, it's easy to respond impulsively, letting emotions dictate our actions. Kathleen and I started practicing the art of pausing before reacting, giving ourselves time to think and reflect before engaging in the conversation.
2. **Use "I" Statements:** Instead of accusing or blaming, we learned to express our feelings using "I" statements. For example, saying "I feel frustrated when…" instead of "You always…" helps keep the conversation focused on the issue rather than attacking the person.
3. **Listen With Intent:** Active listening became a cornerstone of our communication. We made a conscious effort to hear each other out fully before responding, ensuring that both of us felt understood.
4. **Seek Solutions Together:** Rather than arguing about who's right or wrong, we started approaching disagreements as

opportunities to find solutions together. This collaborative mindset helped us shift from conflict to connection.

5. **Apologize and Forgive:** When arguments did occur, we made it a priority to apologize sincerely and forgive each other wholeheartedly. These acts of humility and grace helped us move forward without lingering resentment.

One of the challenges Kathleen and I faced was learning how to manage our emotional responses during disagreements. Yelling, walking away, or giving the cold shoulder might feel satisfying in the moment, but these behaviours only amplify the tension and make resolution harder to achieve.

I've had moments when my frustration led me to raise my voice, thinking that being louder would make my point clearer. Instead, it only made Kathleen feel unheard and overwhelmed. Similarly, when Kathleen withdrew into silence, hoping to avoid further conflict, it left me feeling shut out and disconnected. These emotional responses created barriers to effective communication, turning small disagreements into bigger issues.

We realized that managing our emotions was essential for breaking this cycle. By practicing self-awareness and emotional regulation, we learned to approach conflicts with calmness and clarity. This didn't mean suppressing our feelings—it meant expressing them in ways that invited understanding rather than defensiveness.

Fighting often stems from a desire to "win" the argument or prove a point. Kathleen and I discovered that this mindset—rooted in ego—was one of the biggest obstacles to resolution. When both partners are focused on defending their position, they lose sight of what truly matters: the health of the relationship.

Letting go of ego required humility and a willingness to prioritize our connection over the need to be right. We learned that disagreements are not competitions—they are opportunities to understand each other better. By shifting our focus from winning to listening, we were able to create a space where both of us felt valued and respected.

Kathleen and I also made a commitment to avoid destructive behaviours during conflicts. Raising our voices only intensified the tension and made it harder to communicate effectively. Taking time to cool off is important but walking away without communicating can leave your partner feeling abandoned. Emotional withdrawal creates distance and prevents resolution. Venting to friends or family about disagreements often makes the situation worse, as it involves others in a conflict that should be resolved between partners.

We replaced these behaviours with practices that fostered understanding, such as expressing our feelings calmly, staying present in the conversation, and keeping private matters between us.

Kathleen and I have had to ask ourselves this question: Is the fighting worth the casualty? Every time we've faced a disagreement, we've been reminded that the answer is always no. No argument, no matter how heated, is worth sacrificing the love, respect, and emotional bond that hold a relationship together.

When couples prioritize resolution over conflict, they choose connection over division, love over anger, and growth over resentment. Kathleen and I are living proof of how this choice can transform a relationship, turning moments of tension into opportunities for deeper understanding and trust.

Fighting in relationships, whether verbal, physical, or emotional, comes with significant costs that are never worth the casualty. Kathleen and I learned early in our marriage that disagreements can be navigated without resorting to harmful behaviours. By choosing resolution over conflict, managing our emotional responses, and letting go of ego, we've been able to build a partnership that thrives on mutual respect and love.

As couples face the inevitable challenges of life together, they have the power to choose how they navigate these moments. Will they let fighting define their relationship, or will they rise above it, choosing unity over division? Kathleen and I remain committed to the latter, trusting that this choice will continue to strengthen the bond we share.

AVOID EMOTIONAL BULLYING

WINDOW OF TOLERANCE

Avoid Going From 0-100

A *king and queen* must recognize that their window of tolerance is directly impacted by the weight of their responsibilities and the stress they carry. When obligations pile up, decisions need to be made quickly, and external pressures increase, it becomes easy to go from 0 to 100 in an instant—reacting impulsively rather than responding with wisdom.

Kathleen and I have experienced this firsthand, realizing that when our window of tolerance is small, emotions can escalate, leading to frustration, misunderstandings, and unnecessary tension. We've had to learn that just like rulers who oversee a kingdom, we must pause, process, and regulate our responses, ensuring that stress does not dictate how we treat each other. The key is in recognizing that impulsive reactions may feel justified in the moment, but they do not lead to long-term stability. A wise king and queen know that stepping back, breathing, and addressing obstacles with clarity is far more effective than letting stress take control. Patience protects relationships and understanding preserves unity—whether in marriage or in leadership.

Anger is a natural emotion—one that everyone experiences at some point in life. However, when anger and frustration escalate quickly and uncontrollably, going from "0 to 100" in moments of tension, it can cause lasting damage to relationships, self-esteem, and emotional health. Kathleen and I faced this challenge early in our marriage, particularly because of my temper and "my way or the highway" attitude. At times, I was quick to react when I felt pushed against the wall, fueled by a black-and-white mindset that made compromise difficult. These moments often created a tense environment where Kathleen felt shut out and I felt frustrated by what I saw as resistance to my perspective.

Over time, we realized that these outbursts weren't just harmful to our relationship—they were harmful to us individually and our children. Anger and frustration, especially when unchecked, diminish tolerance, erode trust, and prevent meaningful problem-solving. Kathleen and I committed to understanding the causes of these emotional escalations, the consequences they bring, and the strategies we could use to avoid them. In this chapter, I'll share our journey of addressing the "0 to 100" dynamic, offering insights into why people experience it, the cost it carries, and how couples can move beyond it.

The "0 to 100" escalation—moving from calm to intense anger in seconds—often stems from underlying factors that shape how people react to stress and conflict. For Kathleen and me, this dynamic reflected a mix of personality, upbringing, and emotional triggers. Here are some common reasons why people experience sudden emotional escalations:

1. **Shrinking Window of Tolerance:** Emotional tolerance refers to the capacity to remain calm and composed in stressful situations. When someone's window of tolerance shrinks—due

to fatigue, past trauma, or accumulated stress—small triggers can set off disproportionate reactions.
2. **Feeling Cornered:** People often escalate when they feel pushed against the wall, whether figuratively or literally. This feeling of being trapped or overwhelmed can lead to defensiveness or aggression as a way of protecting oneself.
3. **Rigid Thinking Patterns:** Having a "black-and-white" mindset, like the one I had early in our marriage, can make people less open to other perspectives. When their expectations aren't met, frustration and anger can escalate quickly.
4. **Unresolved Emotional Baggage:** Past experiences, insecurities, and unresolved emotions can act as fuel for sudden outbursts. Kathleen and I found that many of my escalations were tied to feelings of inadequacy or doubt that I hadn't fully addressed.
5. **Impatience and High Expectations:** People who set high expectations for themselves or others may struggle with impatience, reacting strongly when those expectations aren't met.

Understanding these causes gave Kathleen and me insight into why I sometimes went from 0 to 100, helping us identify the root issues we needed to address.

Anger and frustration, when left unchecked, have both immediate and long-term effects that can be damaging—not just to relationships but to overall well-being. Kathleen and I saw this firsthand as my temper led to moments of conflict and emotional exhaustion. Escalating anger can erode trust and intimacy in a relationship. For Kathleen, my outbursts often left her feeling unsafe or disconnected, which weakened our bond.

Chronic anger and frustration take a toll on physical health, increasing blood pressure, heart rate, and stress hormones. These effects

WINDOW OF TOLERANCE

can lead to long-term health issues if not addressed. Intense frustration creates emotional fatigue, leaving people feeling drained and unable to manage future challenges effectively.

When anger takes over, the brain's ability to think clearly and rationally diminishes. Kathleen and I found that during moments of escalation, we were far less able to resolve the issue at hand. Uncontrolled anger often leads to regret, guilt, and feelings of failure, especially when it causes harm to loved ones.

Recognizing these consequences was a turning point for Kathleen and me. We realized that addressing the root causes of escalation wasn't just about saving our relationship—it was about protecting ourselves from the emotional and physical toll it was taking.

The costs of emotional escalation go beyond the immediate reaction. Kathleen and I experienced these negatives firsthand, learning that quick outbursts often created more harm than resolution. Here are some of the most significant downsides:

1. **Broken Communication:** Sudden anger interrupts meaningful dialogue, replacing it with defensiveness or silence. Kathleen often felt she couldn't express herself fully during my outbursts, which led to unresolved issues.
2. **Unintended Hurt:** Words spoken in anger often hurt deeper than intended. Even when apologies are offered later, the emotional scars can linger.
3. **Resentment:** Escalations can breed resentment, especially if they occur repeatedly. Partners may begin to associate negative emotions with the person rather than the issue.
4. **Isolation:** Frequent emotional escalations can create an environment where one partner withdraws, leading to emotional isolation and disconnection.

5. **Reinforcement of Negative Patterns:** When people repeatedly go from 0 to 100, it reinforces a pattern of behaviour that becomes harder to break over time.

Kathleen and I had to face the reality of these costs and make a conscious decision to change our approach. We knew that continuing down this path would jeopardize the love and trust we'd worked so hard to build.

Breaking the cycle of emotional escalation requires intentional effort and practical strategies. Kathleen and I worked on these together, developing tools and habits that helped us manage conflict more effectively. Here are some approaches that can help:

1. **Recognize Your Triggers:** Understanding what sets you off is the first step to avoiding escalation. For me, feeling like I wasn't being heard or understood was a common trigger, and recognizing this helped me address it calmly.
2. **Pause and Reflect:** Taking a moment to breathe and reflect before reacting can prevent impulsive outbursts. Kathleen and I started practicing the "10-second rule," where we'd pause for 10 seconds before responding during tense moments.
3. **Expand Your Window of Tolerance:** Building emotional resilience can help you expand your window of tolerance, making it easier to handle stress without reacting strongly. Techniques like mindfulness, journaling, or prayer can be helpful in developing this skill.
4. **Use "I" Statements:** Expressing your feelings using "I" statements, such as "I feel frustrated when…" instead of "You always…" keeps the conversation constructive.
5. **Focus on Solutions, Not Blame:** Kathleen and I learned to approach disagreements with a mindset of collaboration rather than confrontation. Asking questions like, "How can we solve this together?" shifted the focus from blame to resolution.

6. **Practice Empathy:** Trying to see things from the other person's perspective can help reduce frustration. Kathleen often reminded me that her intentions were never to hurt me but to share her feelings honestly.
7. **Seek Professional Support:** For couples struggling with frequent escalations, therapy or counseling can provide valuable tools and insights for managing conflict.

These strategies helped Kathleen and me transform how we approached disagreements, breaking the cycle of escalation and fostering a healthier dynamic.

One of the challenges I faced was moving away from my "my way or the highway" mindset. This rigid thinking often prevented me from seeing Kathleen's perspective, creating a barrier to effective communication. Over time, I learned to replace black-and-white thinking with flexibility, recognizing that compromise and empathy are essential for a healthy relationship.

Kathleen played a significant role in helping me develop this skill. Her calm and patient nature encouraged me to step back and consider alternative viewpoints, even when they didn't align with my initial expectations. Together, we found ways to blend our perspectives, creating solutions that worked for both of us.

Avoiding the 0 to 100 escalation isn't just about managing anger—it's about choosing connection over conflict, love over frustration, and resolution over resentment. Kathleen and I have learned that the cost of unchecked anger is never worth the damage it causes to a relationship. By recognizing triggers, practicing self-awareness, and approaching disagreements with empathy and collaboration, couples can break free from the cycle of escalation and create a partnership that thrives on trust and respect.

As Kathleen and I continue our journey, we remain committed to building a relationship where communication is constructive, emotions are managed with care, and love remains the guiding force. This commitment has transformed our marriage, showing us that growth and connection are always worth the effort.

WINDOW OF TOLERANCE

As Kathleen and I continue our journey, we remain committed to building a relationship where communication is constructive, reactions are balanced with care, and love remains the guiding force that strengthens the foundation of our marriage, allowing us to grow old together without fear of leaving the window of tolerance.

SHOCK THE BRAIN

Respond With Love Instead of Reacting

Human relationships are complex, filled with moments of connection and understanding but also moments of tension and disagreement. In marriage, these moments can be particularly challenging because they involve deep emotions and shared responsibilities. When disagreements arise, it's easy to fall into the trap of reacting impulsively, saying things that we don't mean and making problems bigger than they actually are. Kathleen and I learned early in our marriage that reacting without processing our thoughts often led to wounds that took time to heal. Words spoken in the heat of the moment have the power to cut deeper than intended, leaving scars that linger long after the argument is over.

To address this challenge, we discovered a powerful tool that transformed how we handle difficult conversations: "shock the brain." It's a concept rooted in interrupting our usual patterns of impulsive reactions and instead choosing responses that reflect love, patience, and understanding. By doing the opposite of what our emotions initially urge us to do, we create a space for resolution rather than escalation and recognizes the consequences of impulsive reactions, and practical ways to approach conflict with intentionality.

Impulsive reactions are often fueled by unfiltered emotions—anger, frustration, disappointment, or hurt. These emotions, while valid, can lead to behaviours that escalate conflicts rather than resolve them. Kathleen and I have experienced firsthand how reacting without processing our thoughts can turn small disagreements into bigger problems.

There were times when Kathleen said something that I found difficult to hear—perhaps a comment about my approach to handing situations that comes up or a suggestion about how to handle a parenting challenge. My initial response was often defensive, fueled by the feeling that I was being criticized. Without taking a moment to process her words, I'd react with statements like, "Why don't you trust me?" or "You always think you know better." These reactions didn't address the issue; instead, they created distance and hurt between us.

Similarly, when I expressed my frustrations bluntly, Kathleen sometimes responded with silence or withdrawal, trying to protect herself from the sting of my words. This dynamic left both of us feeling misunderstood and disconnected, highlighting the need for a different approach.

The consequences of impulsive reactions go beyond the immediate argument. Words spoken in anger can leave deep emotional scars, making it harder to rebuild trust and intimacy. Impulsive reactions often make problems bigger than they need to be, turning a simple disagreement into a heated conflict. When negative behaviours dominate interactions, the emotional bond between partners begins to weaken. After the heat of the moment has passed, many people feel regret for the things they said or did, but the damage has already been done.

Recognizing these consequences was a turning point for Kathleen and me, prompting us to find a better way to navigate conflict.

The concept of "shock the brain" is simple but powerful. It involves interrupting our usual patterns of reacting negatively and instead choosing responses that promote love, understanding, and resolution. Kathleen and I started practicing this technique as a way to break the cycle of impulsive reactions, and it quickly became a cornerstone of how we approach disagreements.

Here's how "shocking the brain" works:

- **Pause and Reframe:** Instead of reacting immediately to a comment or situation, take a moment to pause and reframe your thoughts. Ask yourself, "What's the best way to respond with love in this situation?"
- **Do the Opposite:** If your initial urge is to say something defensive or critical, choose to do the opposite. For example, instead of snapping back at Kathleen when I felt frustrated, I'd hug her or say something kind to reassure her that my feelings weren't about her as a person.
- **Focus on Connection:** Redirect the conversation to focus on the emotional bond rather than the disagreement itself. Kathleen and I often put conversations on hold and shared a cup of tea or coffee, using the break to reconnect before addressing the issue.
- **Lead With Love:** Let love dominate the moment by expressing care, empathy, and understanding. Sometimes, this meant simply saying, "I love you, and I want us to work through this together."

SHOCK THE BRAIN

By shocking the brain, Kathleen and I learned to approach challenges with intentionality rather than impulsivity, creating a safe and supportive environment for problem-solving.

The effectiveness of "shocking the brain" lies in its ability to interrupt negative thought patterns and emotional impulses. When we face conflict, our brains often default to fight-or-flight mode, prioritizing self-protection over connection. This reaction can lead to defensiveness, blame, or withdrawal—all of which make resolution harder to achieve.

By choosing to do the opposite of what our emotions initially urge us to do, we activate the part of the brain responsible for rational thinking and empathy. Instead of fueling the conflict, we create space for understanding and collaboration. Here's why this approach works:

1. **Promotes Emotional Regulation:** Pausing and choosing a thoughtful response helps regulate emotions, preventing the situation from escalating.
2. **Builds Trust:** When partners respond with love and care during moments of tension, it reinforces trust and strengthens the emotional bond.
3. **Encourages Problem-Solving:** Shocking the brain shifts the focus from the conflict itself to finding solutions, making it easier to address the issue constructively.
4. **Deepens Connection:** Expressing love and reassurance during disagreements reminds partners that their relationship is more important than the argument.

Kathleen and I had many opportunities to practice "shocking the brain" in our marriage, particularly during moments of disagreement. Here are some examples of how we used this technique effectively:

1. **Reassuring Each Other During Tough Conversations:** When Kathleen expressed concerns about my decisions, I sometimes

felt defensive. Instead of reacting negatively, I'd pause, take her hand, and say, "I hear what you're saying, and I want us to find a solution together." This small act of reassurance helped diffuse tension and create a collaborative atmosphere.
2. **Taking Breaks During Heated Moments:** If a conversation became too emotional, we'd agree to take a break and do something calming, like sharing a cup of tea. This allowed us to reset emotionally before revisiting the discussion.
3. **Using Physical Touch:** Hugging or holding hands during disagreements helped remind us of our love and commitment, even when our opinions differed.
4. **Expressing Gratitude:** During tense moments, we'd make an effort to express gratitude for each other's perspective, saying things like, "I appreciate you sharing how you feel—it helps me understand you better."

These practices helped us transform conflict into connection, reinforcing the idea that our relationship is stronger than any disagreement.

At the heart of "shocking the brain" is the belief that love should always take priority in a relationship. Kathleen and I learned that disagreements are not battles to be won—they are opportunities to grow and deepen our understanding of each other. By choosing love over negativity, we created a partnership that thrives on mutual respect and empathy.

This approach also taught us that differences in opinions or perceptions are not personal attacks. When Kathleen and I disagreed, we reminded ourselves that our intentions were rooted in love, not in a desire to hurt each other. This mindset made it easier to navigate challenges without letting them dominate our relationship.

One of the key benefits of "shocking the brain" is its ability to prevent negativity and hidden motives from shaping interactions.

SHOCK THE BRAIN

Kathleen and I discovered that unfiltered thoughts often carry unintended messages, such as blame, defensiveness, or resentment. By pausing and choosing thoughtful responses, we avoided these pitfalls and kept our conversations constructive.

If Kathleen said something I found difficult to hear, my initial thought might have been, "She doesn't understand me." Instead of expressing this frustration, I'd choose to say the opposite: "I appreciate you sharing your perspective—it helps me see things differently." This approach not only diffused tension but also strengthened our emotional connection.

"Shocking the brain" is more than just a technique—it's a mindset that transforms how couples navigate conflict. Kathleen and I have learned that by choosing intentional responses over impulsive reactions, we can protect the love, trust, and intimacy that define our relationship. Doing the opposite of what our emotions initially urge us to do has helped us create a partnership that thrives on understanding, empathy, and collaboration.

As couples face the inevitable challenges of marriage, they have the power to choose how they respond. Will they let anger and frustration dictate their interactions, or will they lead with love, creating a space for growth and connection? Kathleen and I remain committed to the latter, trusting that this choice will continue to strengthen the bond we share.

MATURE THE MIND

Build Stronger Relationships Through Growth

A *king and queen* must learn the importance of maturing the mind, understanding that leadership—whether in ruling a kingdom or building a marriage—requires growth, wisdom, and emotional stability. Some rulers step into power at a young age, and though they may carry the title of king or queen for decades, if they fail to develop their mindset, they will continue to make impulsive, immature decisions that do not serve their people—or their relationships—well.

Kathleen and I have come to realize that to stand as a king and rule as a queen, you must cultivate a mature perspective. Reacting to situations as though we were teenagers—driven by emotion rather than wisdom—would only create instability in our marriage and family. We've seen firsthand that growth requires intentional effort, allowing life's experiences to refine us, shape our character, and make us better leaders for those we love. Our children, our family, and the generations to come depend on the maturity we embrace today, ensuring that we lead with wisdom rather than emotion and build a legacy rooted in strength, love, and faith.

If a glass of milk falls and breaks, you could get angry, question why it happened, assign blame, and offer explanations—but none of that will bring the glass back to its original state. Children often justify their actions by explaining why things happened, using reasoning as a way to defend themselves. But as adults, we need to shift our focus from explanations to problem-solving. Instead of dwelling on *why* the glass broke, the real question should be: "What can we do to prevent it from breaking again?"

Kings and queens understand this principle well—they don't get stuck in the past; they problem-solve and move forward. Kathleen and I have learned that when challenges arise in life or marriage, fixating on blame only drains energy, while proactive thinking strengthens relationships. Solutions create progress, while over-explaining keeps us stuck. A wise ruler, like a wise couple, knows that growth comes from learning, adjusting, and moving forward, not reliving what has already been broken. It moved from "I" to "We."

Relationships evolve over time, shaped by the experiences, challenges, and milestones that couples face together. As this evolution unfolds, maturity becomes the cornerstone of a healthy, thriving partnership. Maturing the mind goes beyond age; it involves gaining wisdom, learning from the past, and embracing growth. Sadly, some couples, even after decades together, remain stuck in the mindset and behaviours they had when they first got married, focusing on weaknesses rather than appreciating the growth they've acquired along the way.

Kathleen and I often reflect on our journey, talking about how we used to react to challenges—how we disciplined our children, how we managed disagreements, and how insecurities shaped the rules we imposed in our early years. But as time went on, we learned the importance of tapping into the maturity we've gained, transforming our relationship through confidence, trust, acceptance, and wisdom.

Maturing the mind allows couples to move beyond surface-level frustrations and embrace deeper emotional connections. It empowers partners to focus on what truly matters, letting go of unproductive habits and unrealistic expectations. Kathleen and I discovered the beauty of accepting each other for who we are rather than trying to mould one another into an idealized version of perfection inspired by magazines or movies. Through this journey of growth, we learned that maturity is not just about accumulating years—it's about actively choosing to grow, adapt, and deepen the bond we share.

The purpose of maturing the mind is to move beyond reactive thinking and embrace thoughtful, intentional behaviour. It involves developing the emotional intelligence and self-awareness needed to navigate challenges without resorting to conflict, blame, or frustration. For Kathleen and me, maturing the mind meant learning how to process situations with grace, patience, and perspective. Instead of reacting impulsively or dwelling on weaknesses, we learned to focus on solutions, mutual understanding, and growth.

In relationships, the immature mind often clings to insecurities, rigid expectations, and the desire to "win" disagreements. This mindset creates tension, as partners struggle to meet unrealistic standards or feel inadequate. Kathleen and I found that these tendencies were especially prevalent during the early years of our marriage, when we were still adjusting to life as a couple and figuring out how to balance our individual needs with our shared goals.

Maturing the mind allows couples to move past these obstacles. It invites them to embrace vulnerability, trust their partner's intentions, and prioritize the health of the relationship over the need to be right. The purpose of maturity is not to eliminate challenges—it's to approach them with wisdom and resilience, turning potential conflicts into opportunities for growth.

Maturing the mind brings immense value to relationships, enhancing emotional connection, trust, and fulfillment. Kathleen and I have seen firsthand how this growth has transformed our marriage. Here are some of the key benefits we've experienced:

Maturity fosters trust by reducing insecurity and doubt. As Kathleen and I grew in confidence and dependency on each other, we built a foundation of trust that allowed us to navigate challenges without questioning each other's commitment.

Early in our marriage, we often tried to "fix" each other, hoping to mould the other person into the perfect partner. Over time, we learned to embrace each other's unique qualities, seeing differences not as obstacles but as strengths that enrich our relationship.

Maturity helps couples move beyond surface-level communication and engage in meaningful dialogue. Kathleen and I learned to focus on what's truly important, choosing discussions that strengthen our bond rather than dwelling on minor irritations.

Mature minds approach conflict with a spirit of collaboration, recognizing that disagreements are natural and can lead to deeper understanding. By learning which battles are worth fighting and which can be let go, Kathleen and I reduced the tension in our relationship and found greater harmony.

Maturity deepens emotional intimacy, allowing couples to connect on a deeper level. Kathleen and I found that accepting each other for who we are created a sense of unity that transcends superficial differences.

One of the most significant ways maturity transforms relationships is by shifting the focus from weaknesses to strengths. Early in our marriage, Kathleen and I often found ourselves fixated on each other's flaws. If I made a decision she didn't agree with or if she approached a situation differently than I would have, frustration would sometimes take over. These moments were fueled by our insecurities and the belief that our perspectives were the "right" ones.

But as we matured, we learned to see the value in each other's approaches. Kathleen's thoughtful, deliberate nature complemented my action-oriented style, creating a balance that allowed us to tackle challenges more effectively. Instead of dwelling on weaknesses, we began celebrating the strengths that each of us brought to the relationship.

Maturity also helped us let go of unrealistic expectations. Early on, we often compared ourselves to idealized images of couples we saw in movies or magazines, hoping to emulate their perfection. This mindset led to unnecessary pressure and dissatisfaction, as we felt we were falling short of the standards we'd set for ourselves. Through maturity, we realized that perfection is an illusion—what matters most is authenticity, mutual respect, and love.

One of the hallmarks of maturing the mind is the ability to learn from mistakes. Kathleen and I made plenty of them, especially in the early years of our marriage. We were quick to argue, slow to forgive, and often stuck in our own ways. These behaviours created tension that occasionally left us feeling disconnected.

What changed was our willingness to reflect on these moments and grow from them. Instead of seeing mistakes as failures, we began viewing them as opportunities for growth. For example, if we had a disagreement about disciplining the children, we'd take time afterward to discuss what went wrong and how we could approach similar situations differently in the future. These conversations were challenging at times, but they helped us develop a stronger sense of teamwork and understanding.

MATURE THE MIND

Learning from mistakes also required humility—a willingness to admit when we were wrong and to seek forgiveness when necessary. Kathleen and I learned that maturity isn't about always having the answers—it's about being open to growth, even when it's uncomfortable.

Maturing the mind is a lifelong process, but there are practical steps couples can take to cultivate this growth in their relationship. Kathleen and I have found the following practices especially helpful:

1. **Reflect on Growth:** Take time to reflect on how your relationship has evolved over the years. Celebrate the progress you've made and use it as motivation to continue growing.
2. **Embrace Vulnerability:** Allow yourself to be vulnerable with your partner, sharing your fears, insecurities, and aspirations. Vulnerability strengthens emotional intimacy and builds trust.
3. **Focus on Strengths:** Shift your focus from weaknesses to strengths, acknowledging the unique qualities that each partner brings to the relationship.
4. **Prioritize Communication:** Choose discussions that enhance your connection, focusing on what truly matters rather than dwelling on minor irritations.
5. **Let Go of Unrealistic Expectations:** Release the pressure to emulate perfection and instead embrace authenticity. Accept your partner for who they are, valuing their individuality.
6. **Learn From Mistakes:** View mistakes as opportunities for growth rather than failures. Reflect on what went wrong, seek solutions, and commit to doing better in the future.
7. **Practice Forgiveness:** Let go of resentment and choose forgiveness, creating a space for healing and reconciliation.

Maturing the mind is a journey that transforms relationships, turning them into partnerships rooted in trust, acceptance, and love. Kathleen and I have experienced this growth firsthand, learning to navigate challenges with wisdom, celebrate each other's strengths, and let go of unrealistic expectations. Through maturity, we've built a relationship that is resilient, fulfilling, and deeply connected.

For couples looking to strengthen their bond, maturing the mind offers a powerful pathway to growth. By choosing to reflect, embrace vulnerability, and prioritize love, partners can create a relationship that stands strong through the test of time. Kathleen and I remain committed to this journey, trusting that maturity will continue to shape our partnership and deepen the love we share.

MATURE THE MIND

A FILING CARBINET

Build Positive Memory Cards

The human brain is an extraordinary organ, capable of storing and organizing vast amounts of information. Kathleen and I often reflect on the metaphor of the brain as a filing cabinet, where every experience, thought, and emotion is categorized and stored as a "memory card" for later use. Over the years, we've come to understand the importance of curating what we place in this metaphorical filing cabinet. The experiences we choose to remember—whether positive or negative—shape how we perceive ourselves, our relationships, and the world around us.

In our marriage, we've learned to prioritize creating positive memory cards. This isn't about ignoring challenges or pretending that life is always perfect—it's about intentionally focusing on the moments that bring joy, connection, and growth. By storing more positive cards than negative ones, we've created a foundation of love and resilience that allows us to face challenges with hope and gratitude. We've even likened the process to learning a new language, where every positive memory becomes a new "word" in the vocabulary of love and understanding.

Think of your brain as a giant filing cabinet, where every experience is stored as a "memory card." Some of these cards are filled with joy, laughter, and love, while others capture moments of pain, frustration, or loss. Every time you encounter a situation, your brain instinctively pulls a card from the cabinet to inform your reaction. For Kathleen and me, this metaphor became a powerful tool for understanding how our past experiences shaped our interactions in the present.

Early in our marriage, we realized that many of our reactions to disagreements were influenced by negative memory cards. If Kathleen expressed her concern, my brain might pull a card labeled "criticism," even if her intentions were rooted in care and collaboration. Similarly, if I raised a parenting concern, Kathleen's brain might retrieve a card labeled "pressure," even if I was simply trying to brainstorm solutions.

These negative cards often led to misunderstandings, making it harder for us to connect or resolve issues. But as we worked on our relationship, we discovered the power of intentionally creating and storing positive memory cards. By focusing on moments of joy, affirmation, and love, we began replacing the negative cards with positive ones, transforming how we approached challenges.

Building positive memory cards is not just about capturing happy moments—it's about intentionally creating experiences that reinforce love, trust, and connection. Kathleen and I found that these cards became a valuable resource during difficult times, reminding us of the strength and beauty of our relationship.

Here are some ways we've worked to create positive memory cards:

1. **Celebrate Small Wins:** Whether it's achieving a financial goal, overcoming a parenting challenge, or simply surviving a

stressful week, we take time to celebrate the small victories. These moments remind us of our resilience and teamwork.

2. **Prioritize Quality Time:** Shared experiences, like date nights, family outings, or quiet evenings at home, become the foundation for positive memory cards. Kathleen and I make it a priority to nurture these moments, knowing they'll be stored in the cabinet for years to come.

3. **Express Gratitude:** Saying "thank you" and acknowledging each other's efforts reinforces appreciation and love. Every act of gratitude becomes a positive card that strengthens our emotional connection.

4. **Choose Love Over Anger:** During disagreements, we make a conscious effort to lead with love rather than frustration. These moments of kindness and understanding create cards that remind us of the strength of our bond.

By intentionally creating positive memory cards, Kathleen and I have built a filing cabinet filled with joy and resilience, allowing us to face challenges with hope and gratitude.

No one can avoid negative experiences entirely—they're a natural part of life. But Kathleen and I learned that while negative cards might make their way into the filing cabinet, we have the power to ensure that positive cards outnumber them. This balance is crucial for maintaining emotional health and fostering strong relationships.

When negative cards dominate, they shape how we perceive ourselves, our partners, and our circumstances. We might feel stuck in patterns of resentment, insecurity, or pessimism, making it harder to grow or connect. Kathleen and I saw this dynamic early in our marriage, when disagreements sometimes overshadowed the love we shared.

Shifting the balance required intentional effort. We began focusing on positive moments, expressing gratitude, and celebrating each other's strengths. Over time, the positive cards began to outnumber the negative ones, transforming how we viewed our relationship. Today, even during tough times, we can pull from the cabinet and find cards filled with love, support, and affirmation.

Research highlights the importance of cultivating positivity, noting that individuals who focus on positive experiences are more likely to experience emotional resilience and well-being (Fredrickson, 2013).

For Kathleen and me, storing positive cards became a practice of choosing joy and gratitude, even in the face of challenges.

Creating and storing positive memory cards is like learning a new language—a language of love, gratitude, and understanding. Just as language learning requires practice and intentionality, building positivity in relationships requires consistent effort. For Kathleen and me, this meant rewiring how we approached interactions, replacing negative patterns with affirming ones.

One example of this transformation came during moments of disagreement. Instead of focusing on what went wrong or assigning blame, we learned to express appreciation for each other's perspectives. This shift in tone changed the dynamic of our conversations, creating positive memory cards that reinforced collaboration rather than division.

Just as learning a language involves repetition and immersion, building positivity requires ongoing commitment. Kathleen and I found that the more we practiced gratitude, affirmation, and connection, the more natural it became to approach challenges with hope and resilience.

One of the most powerful ways to create positive memory cards is by tapping into the five senses—smelling, touching, tasting, hearing, and seeing. Engaging the senses enhances experiences, making them more vivid and memorable. Kathleen and I discovered that intentionally using the senses during moments of connection deepened our emotional bond and created lasting memories.

Here's how we've incorporated the senses into our relationship:

1. **Smelling:** Certain scents, like a favorite perfume or the aroma of home-cooked meals, evoke powerful memories. Kathleen and I often use candles or essential oils to create an inviting atmosphere that reminds us of comforting moments.
2. **Touching:** Physical touch, whether it's holding hands, hugging, or cuddling, reinforces emotional connection. Kathleen and I make it a priority to use touch as a way to express love and reassurance.
3. **Tasting:** Sharing meals together creates opportunities for connection, whether it's cooking a favourite recipe or trying something new. Food becomes a way to celebrate and create positive memory cards.
4. **Hearing:** Music, laughter, and kind words all contribute to positive experiences. Kathleen and I often use music to set the tone for our evenings, creating an atmosphere of relaxation and joy.
5. **Seeing:** Visual experiences, like family photos or beautiful landscapes, reinforce positive memories. Kathleen and I enjoy capturing moments through photography, preserving the joy of shared experiences.

By engaging the senses, Kathleen and I have enriched our relationship and created a filing cabinet filled with vivid, positive memories. Building a filing cabinet filled with positive memory cards requires intentional effort and thoughtful practices. Here are some strategies Kathleen and I have found helpful:

1. **Focus on Gratitude:** Make it a habit to express gratitude daily, whether it's for your partner's efforts, a shared experience, or a small victory.

A FILING CARBINET

2. **Celebrate Together:** Take time to celebrate milestones, achievements, and everyday moments of joy. These celebrations create lasting positive memory cards.
3. **Engage the Senses:** Use the five senses to enhance experiences and create vivid, memorable moments.
4. **Shift Perspective:** When faced with challenges, focus on solutions rather than problems. This mindset creates positive cards that reinforce resilience.
5. **Prioritize Connection:** Make quality time a priority, using shared experiences to strengthen the emotional bond and create positive memories.

The metaphor of the brain as a filing cabinet reminds us of the power we have to shape our perceptions and experiences. Kathleen and I have learned that by intentionally creating and storing positive memory cards, we can build a foundation of love, trust, and resilience that carries us through life's challenges.

Tapping into the five senses, learning the language of positivity, and focusing on what truly matters has transformed our relationship, creating a legacy of joy and connection. As couples navigate their journey together, they have the opportunity to curate their filing cabinet, ensuring that the cards they store reflect the beauty and strength of their partnership. Kathleen and I remain committed to this practice, trusting that the memories we create will continue to inspire and uplift us for years to come.

PUT CLOSURE TO YOUR PAST

Let Go and Move On

A *king and queen* must recognize that with the weight of leadership comes countless decisions, and inevitably, some will be wrong. They may enter a marriage carrying baggage from their past—patterns learned from their families, wounds from previous experiences, and insecurities that surface in moments of stress. And when pressure mounts, the mind has a way of magnifying mistakes, feeding intrusive thoughts that chip away at self-confidence and unity.

Kathleen and I have learned that without putting closure to the past, it continues to affect the present. The only way to rule wisely, love freely, and build a marriage that withstands challenges is to let go, move forward, and refuse to let old wounds weaken the foundation we've built.

A kingdom cannot thrive if its rulers are constantly weighed down by regrets and unresolved burdens. We had to release the past, learn from it, and choose love, growth, and healing over the weight of yesterday. That is how a marriage, like a kingdom, stands strong—through wisdom, resilience, and the courage to move forward.

One of the most challenging yet transformative journeys in life is learning to move on from the past. For Kathleen and me, this process has been essential to growing as a couple and building the strong, unified foundation we share today. Like many couples, we have faced mistakes, wrong choices, and moments of pain that could have defined our story. However, we realized that holding onto these experiences only served to weigh us down, limiting our potential and preventing us from thriving in our roles as husband and wife. Moving on required us to defuse the stress that came with past struggles, put closure to the mistakes we made, and embrace a new chapter filled with growth, maturity, and purpose.

Moving forward is not about ignoring the past—it's about learning from it, forgiving yourself and others, and choosing to live fully in the present. It's a process of detaching yourself from old wounds, creating space for gratitude, avoiding triggers, and maintaining positive thinking. It's about choosing to stand tall as a king and rule with grace as a queen, mastering your roles and responsibilities as you build a life of love and resilience.

Stress, especially when tied to unresolved issues, can have a profound impact on a relationship. Kathleen and I have experienced firsthand how the stress of past mistakes or unresolved disagreements can linger, creating tension that disrupts the harmony we strive to maintain. Over time, we learned that defusing stress is the first step to moving on—it creates the emotional clarity and space needed to address underlying issues and move forward with a fresh perspective.

One of the strategies we've used to defuse stress is practicing mindfulness. When the weight of past struggles felt overwhelming, we'd take a moment to pause, breathe, and focus on the present. This simple practice reminded us that the past no longer has power over us unless we allow it to. By focusing on the here and now, we were able to release stress and approach challenges with a calmer, more balanced mindset.

Another way we've worked to defuse stress is by prioritizing self-care. Whether it's taking a walk together, enjoying a quiet evening at home, or simply sharing a cup of tea, these moments of connection allowed us to reset and recharge. Defusing stress isn't about avoiding the past—it's about creating the emotional stability needed to face it with courage and clarity.

Closure is a vital part of moving on. It's the process of acknowledging what has happened, learning from it, and choosing to let it go. For Kathleen and me, putting closure to the past meant addressing unresolved issues and making a conscious decision to stop carrying them into the present.

One of the most important steps we took was having honest conversations about the mistakes we made and the lessons we learned. These conversations weren't always easy—they required vulnerability, humility, and a willingness to confront uncomfortable truths. But they also created a space for healing and reconciliation, allowing us to move forward without the baggage of old wounds.

We also learned that closure isn't just about addressing external conflicts—it's about making peace with ourselves. This meant forgiving ourselves for the wrong choices we'd made and recognizing that our mistakes didn't define us. For me, this process involved letting go of the guilt I felt for past decisions that caused stress in our relationship. For Kathleen, it meant releasing the burden of self-doubt and embracing her worth as a partner and a person.

By putting closure to the past, we freed ourselves from its hold, creating space for growth and renewal.

PUT CLOSURE TO YOUR PAST

Forgiveness is one of the most powerful tools for moving on. Without it, the past can remain a source of pain, resentment, and division. For Kathleen and me, forgiveness was a turning point in our journey. It allowed us to rebuild trust, restore our emotional connection, and create a foundation of grace and understanding.

Forgiving each other required us to focus on the bigger picture of our relationship. We reminded ourselves that we were both human—imperfect but committed to growing and learning together. When conflicts arose, we chose to approach them with empathy, seeking to understand each other's perspectives rather than assigning blame. This mindset made it easier to extend forgiveness, even when emotions were raw.

Forgiving ourselves, however, was often the harder task. It's easy to replay mistakes in your mind, dwelling on what you could have done differently. But Kathleen and I learned that self-forgiveness is essential for personal growth. By accepting our imperfections and choosing to move forward, we were able to release the guilt and shame that once held us back.

Moving on also requires detaching yourself from the issues that once consumed your thoughts and emotions. This doesn't mean ignoring or minimizing them—it means recognizing that these issues no longer define your present or dictate your future. For Kathleen and me, detaching from past struggles meant shifting our focus from problems to possibilities.

One of the ways we achieved this was by creating new routines and habits that reinforced positivity and growth. For example, instead of revisiting old arguments or rehashing past mistakes, we'd spend time planning for the future, setting goals for our family, and celebrating our progress. These activities helped us redirect our energy toward building a better tomorrow.

Detachment also involved setting boundaries around negative thought patterns. When I found myself dwelling on a past mistake, I'd consciously remind myself that the situation had been resolved and no longer needed my attention. Kathleen used similar techniques, choosing to focus on gratitude and affirmations rather than letting old doubts resurface.

One transformative practices Kathleen and I adopted was creating a gratitude journal. This simple habit allowed us to focus on the blessings in our lives rather than the challenges we faced. Each day, we'd take a few moments to write down things we were grateful for—whether it was a kind word, a small victory, or a shared moment of laughter.

The gratitude journal became a powerful tool for shifting our mindset. It reminded us that even in difficult times, there was always something to be thankful for. It reminded us to pray for the unresolved issues and to give praise and thanks to God for issues resolved. This practice not only strengthened our bond as a couple but also helped us cultivate a sense of joy and contentment that carried us through life's ups and downs.

Research shows that practicing gratitude can improve mental health, enhance relationships, and increase overall well-being (Wood et al., 2018). For Kathleen and me, the gratitude journal was a way to anchor ourselves in positivity, creating a foundation for moving forward with hope and resilience.

Part of moving on is recognizing and avoiding the triggers that can pull you back into old patterns of thinking and behaviour. For Kathleen and me, this meant identifying the situations, habits, or thoughts that reignited past pain and making a conscious effort to steer clear of them.

If a particular topic of conversation consistently led to tension, we'd agree to approach it differently or discuss it at a later time when emotions weren't as heightened. If a specific behaviour reminded one of us of a past conflict, we'd address it with empathy and understanding, focusing on finding solutions rather than assigning blame.

Avoiding triggers isn't about avoiding reality—it's about creating a safe and supportive environment where healing and growth can take place. By minimizing exposure to negative influences, Kathleen and I were able to focus on building a stronger, healthier relationship.

Positive thinking played a crucial role in helping Kathleen and me move on from the past. By choosing to focus on possibilities rather than limitations, we were able to approach challenges with a sense of hope and determination.

One of the ways we cultivated positive thinking was by reframing our perspective on mistakes and setbacks. Instead of viewing them as failures, we saw them as opportunities for growth and learning. This shift in mindset allowed us to approach challenges with resilience, knowing that every experience contributed to our journey.

We also made an effort to surround ourselves with positivity, whether it was through uplifting conversations, inspirational reading, or acts of kindness. These influences reinforced our commitment to maintaining a positive outlook, even during difficult times.

As Kathleen and I matured in our roles as husband and wife, we realized the importance of standing as a king and ruling as a queen in our relationship. We had to let go in order to be effective and make wise decisions. We developed mental toughness and stop the concepts of being a victim.

For me, standing as a king meant leading with integrity, protecting our family, and setting the tone for our shared values. For Kathleen, ruling as a queen meant nurturing our relationships, creating stability, and offering wisdom and guidance. Together, we balanced these roles, recognizing that our strengths complemented each other and allowed us to navigate life's challenges with grace.

By embracing these roles, we were able to move on from the past and focus on building a future filled with love, trust, and purpose. We learned that mistakes, wrong choices, and bad decisions didn't define us—they were stepping stones on the path to growth and maturity.

Moving on is a journey of defusing stress, putting closure to the past, and choosing to live fully in the present. Kathleen and I have learned that forgiveness, gratitude, and positive thinking are powerful tools for releasing the hold of the past and embracing the possibilities of the future. By detaching ourselves from old wounds, avoiding triggers, and focusing on our roles as partners, we've built a relationship that thrives

PUT CLOSURE TO YOUR PAST

CONCLUSION

As we reach the final pages of *Stand As A King and Rule As A Queen,* we hope that the journey through these chapters has provided wisdom, encouragement, and practical insights to help you build a thriving relationship. Marriage, like any kingdom, is built through intentional choices, trust, accountability, and a willingness to embrace both the joys and challenges of life together.

Kathleen and I have walked this path for over three decades, and every lesson we have shared in this book is rooted in experience—both the successes and the struggles. We did not arrive at a strong marriage by chance; we built it, brick by brick, through communication, respect, and unwavering commitment to each other. As we reflect on the wisdom gained through the years, we recognize that marriage is not about perfection but perseverance.

Standing as a king and ruling as a queen is not a mindset of dominance or power—it is a call to lead, nurture, and strengthen your relationship through unity. It is about recognizing that two are better than one, working together with a shared vision, and understanding that

CONCLUSION

your labor will bear good returns when built on mutual trust and responsibility.

Throughout this journey, we've explored the significance of roles within a relationship and the common question that many couples struggle with—who is more important? The truth is, both are equally vital, each contributing unique strengths to the foundation of the relationship. A king brings vision, protection, and stability; a queen provides wisdom, nurture, and emotional depth. One cannot thrive without the other, and when both embrace their responsibilities without competition or resentment, the marriage flourishes.

Couples who recognize the importance of identifying what they can and cannot do allow themselves to lean on each other's strengths rather than wasting energy fighting battles they were never meant to take on alone. Marriage is about complementing, not controlling, and when both individuals appreciate their partner's gifts and contributions, they unlock the power of ruling together with wisdom.

One of the most beautiful aspects of marriage is the coming together of two distinct individuals—each with unique personalities, perspectives, and approaches to life. Yet many couples struggle because they have not learned how to appreciate characters and personalities or embrace differences as strengths rather than weaknesses.

Kathleen and I are different in many ways. I lean towards assertiveness and action, while she approaches decisions with quiet reflection. Early in our marriage, these differences caused tension, but over time, we realized that our differences strengthened our relationship rather than weakened it. By learning to respect each other's perspectives, we cultivated a team mindset, recognizing that together, we achieve far more than we ever could alone.

Unity in leadership means ruling together as a team, holding each other accountable, and prioritizing trust. Accountability is not about blame—it is about transparency. Healthy couples recognize that when trust is maintained, both individuals feel empowered and secure in their roles.

Every marriage faces difficulties. Financial worries, disagreements, emotional wounds, and unexpected life challenges all have the potential to divide couples if not handled with maturity. We learned that the key to overcoming struggles is separating the problem from the person. Instead of seeing our spouse as the "cause" of frustration, we worked together to problem-solve and address the root issues.

Part of this process means recognizing that you will not always see things eye to eye, but agreeing to disagree with respect is a powerful tool for maintaining harmony. No two people will think exactly alike, and rather than forcing agreement, couples must learn how to hear each other, respect differing viewpoints, and find compromises that strengthen their unity.

One of the great challenges in relationships is learning how to balance emotional reactions with rational thought. Some individuals process things deeply and emotionally, while others approach challenges with logical solutions. Neither approach is wrong, but failing to appreciate these differences can create unnecessary conflict.

Kathleen and I learned that emotion and reason must work together, not against each other. By acknowledging our natural tendencies and making space for both perspectives, we created a balanced dynamic where both hearts and minds are valued.

Nothing in life is wasted. Every challenge, every moment of pressure, every mistake—each contributes to growth and maturity. Couples who recognize that pressure refines rather than destroys allow themselves to use struggles as fuel for strengthening their relationship.

Kathleen and I have experienced this transformation firsthand. Experience and maturity shaped how we interact, making us more

CONCLUSION

patient, understanding, and confident in our ability to navigate difficulties. Nothing is wasted when you choose to grow from it.

One of the greatest risks in relationships is allowing problems to dominate instead of love leading the way. Couples who focus more on what is wrong rather than what is right tend to create an environment of frustration rather than connection.

We discovered that avoiding an eggshell environment, preventing emotional bullying, and learning how to avoid going from 0 to 100 in emotional responses helped us cultivate a relationship built on security rather than fear.

Love must rule over conflict, ensuring that disagreements never overshadow commitment.

A powerful lesson Kathleen and I learned is the importance of shocking the brain—choosing to respond with love rather than reacting impulsively. Many fights could be avoided if couples took a moment to pause, breathe, and choose a response rooted in care rather than frustration.

Instead of speaking harsh words, choose kindness. Instead of shutting down, engage thoughtfully. These small choices transform relationships, strengthening emotional bonds and building deeper trust.

Relationships are built through memories—not just the major milestones but the small, everyday moments. Couples who choose to build positive memory cards cultivate an environment where gratitude and appreciation are abundant.

Kathleen and I learned the value of documenting our joys, ensuring that even in hard times, we had a foundation of positivity to rely on. Our minds are like filing cabinets, and what we choose to store impacts how we experience love.

Finally, one of the most important aspects of a thriving marriage is learning to let go. Holding onto past mistakes, resentments, or guilt can create walls that prevent real intimacy. We have learned to put closure to the past, forgive ourselves and each other, and move forward with faith and purpose.

Every couple must make a conscious decision to focus on the present and future rather than being weighed down by old burdens.

Marriage is a kingdom built on trust, teamwork, and love. When couples embrace their roles, complement each other, and rule together, they create a legacy that withstands the test of time.

Kathleen and I encourage every couple to choose love daily, commit to growing together, and stand firm in their roles as king and queen, ruling with wisdom, grace, and strength.

Your kingdom awaits—rule it well, and let love lead the way.

CONCLUSION

REFERENCES

Barton, A. W., Futris, T. G., & Bradford, A. B. (2021). The connection between shared relationship goals and marital satisfaction: A longitudinal study. *Journal of Family Psychology, 35*(2), 204–215.

Braun, S., Cugueró-Escofet, N., & Wittrock, J. (2018). Leadership and teams: Finding the sweet spot of collaboration. *Frontiers in Psychology*, 9, 1691.

Cain, S. (2012). *Quiet: The power of introverts in a world that can't stop talking.* Crown Publishing Group.

DeChurch, L. A., & Mesmer-Magnus, J. R. (2010). The cognitive underpinnings of effective teamwork: A meta-analysis. *Journal of Applied Psychology*, 95(1), 32–53.

Edmondson, A. C. (2019). *The fearless organization: Creating psychological safety in the workplace for learning, innovation, and growth.* Wiley.

Eggerichs, E. (2020). *Love and Respect: The love she most desires; The respect he desperately needs.* Thomas

REFERENCES

Emmons, R. A., & McCullough, M. E. (2021). The psychology of gratitude and its role in relationships. *Journal of Positive Psychology*, 16(3), 247–258.

Finkel, E. J., Simpson, J. A., & Eastwick, P. W. (2017). The psychology of close relationships: Four key questions and new findings. *Annual Review of Psychology, 68*, 383–411.

Fredrickson, B. L. (2013). Positive emotions broaden and build. *Advances in Experimental Social Psychology*, 47, 1–53.

Gottman, J. M., & Silver, N. (1999). *The seven principles for making marriage work: A practical guide from the country's foremost relationship expert.* Crown Publishers.

Gottman, J., & Silver, N. (2019). *The seven principles for making marriage work: A practical guide from the country's foremost relationship expert.* Harmony.

Hatfield, E., & Rapson, R. L. (1993). *Love, sex, and intimacy: Their psychology, biology, and history.* HarperCollins College Publishers.

Helgoe, L. A. (2020). *Introvert power: Why your inner life is your hidden strength.* Sourcebooks.

Markman, H. J., & Rhoades, G. K. (2020). Relationship quality and its challenges in modern marriages: A decade in review. *Journal of Marriage and Family, 82*(4), 1459–1473.

Roberts, B. W., Luo, J., Briley, D. A., Chow, P. I., & Hill, P. L. (2020). A critical review of personality development research. *Annual Review of Psychology*, 71, 547-577.

Van Knippenberg, D., van Ginkel, W. P., & Homan, A. C. (2020). Diversity mindsets and the performance of diverse teams. *Organizational Behavior and Human Decision Processes*, 159, 92–104.